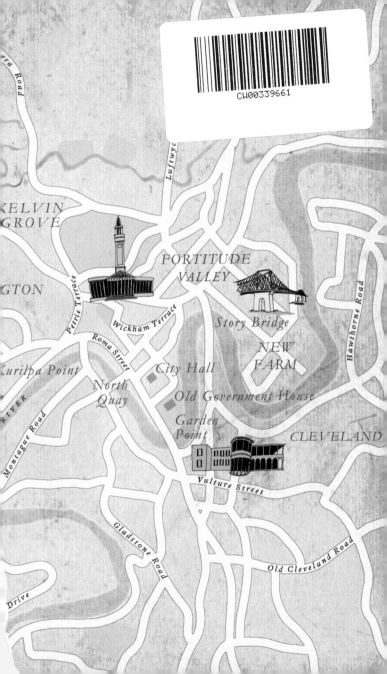

Brisbane

Brisbane

MATTHEW CONDON

NEW
SOUTH

A New South book

Published by
University of New South Wales Press Ltd
University of New South Wales
Sydney NSW 2052
AUSTRALIA
www.unswpress.com.au

National Library of Australia
Cataloguing-in-Publication entry
    Author: Condon, Matthew (Matthew Steven), 1962–
    Title: Brisbane/Matthew Condon.
    ISBN: 978 1 74223 028 3 (hbk.)
    Notes: Includes index.
      Bibliography.
    Subjects: Condon, Matthew (Matthew Steven), 1962 – Homes
      and haunts.
      Brisbane (Qld.) – Description and travel.
      Brisbane (Qld.) – History.
      Brisbane (Qld.) – Social life and customs.
      Brisbane (Qld.) – Biography.
Dewey Number: 994.31

Design Josephine Pajor-Markus
Cover design gogoGingko
Cover image Ben Ryan
Author photo Russell Shakespeare
Endpaper map David Atkinson, handmademaps.com
Printer Everbest

For
my children
Bridie Rose and Finnigan

'And you really live by the river? What a jolly life!'

'By it and with it and on it and in it,' said the Rat. 'It's brother and sister to me, and aunts, and company, and food and drink, and (naturally) washing. It's my world, and I don't want any other.'

Kenneth Grahame, *The Wind in the Willows*

And now cometh he from the depths of the sea,
To survey the point where the town is to be;
But sadly trepann'd — two miles from dry land —
He drives his poor snout in the treacherous sand.
'Is this your fine town?' says the whale with a frown …

By Quiz, *The Moreton Bay Courier*, 17 July 1847

Then one day the boy started building a replica of his own city under the house.

There was meagre light down there, in the shadowed wedge, but on summer mornings little knives and coins of it flashed through the *Monstera deliciosa* and spoon lilies that grew at the sides of the small box-shaped colonial. Things lived in that dark space and left curious tracks in the soil. And at the approach of violent afternoon thunderstorms that rolled in from the west across the ranges, the sloped earth seemed to hold its breath, the elephant-eared plants trembled, and it quickly became cold and gloomy.

The boy was too young to work from maps. In the few years he'd been sentient to the world around him, much of what he knew about the city he'd seen from the broad open windows of trams on excursions with his grandmother, through the grime of school bus windows, from the back of the family's old Holden station wagon. He was aware of the memorial to the city's founder, had been across the river, and been walked by the hand through King George Square in front of the city hall and looked up at its clock tower. The first time he heard the massive clock strike the hour it felt like the start of his life.

So he began his replica city with the clock. He used an old timber off-cut for the tower, and drew wobbly faces and hands on its four sides, adequate but hardly reflecting the city hall proper, that beautifully creamy, sandstone centre to his universe with its green lions guarding the heavy bronze doors, its grand columns, its auditorium beneath a monstrous copper dome, and the imposing tower with, at its tip, an illuminated globe that shone on the clouds at night. He liked the way the shadow thrown by the tower moved over the nearby buildings and streets like a sundial. Every time he looked at his handmade clock tower he remembered how the vibrations of the bell quivered through your body and how, as he understood later, that very moment in time, the time of your city, passed into you.

Street grids emanated from the base of his hokey clock tower, broad enough for a Matchbox car, and with other bits of wood and discarded seedling containers he reproduced some of the city buildings he knew — the McDonnell & East department store, the Regent Cinema, the Treasury, the Bellevue Hotel, Parliament House, the Museum, Cloudland and the Black Cat Casket Agency, with its string of sneaky felines on the shopfront awning.

Next came the serpentine river, a muddy, twisting, restless thing that pushed out into the bay with its own sort of languid apathy. This was a river simply to be crossed. It offered no poetry. It was illegible and dangerous. From its source in the mountains, its path to the coast was gently wriggly at the beginning, but by the time it approached the city it took wild perambulations, before it straightened out and relaxed closer to its mouth.

This was a river the boy lazily squiggled through his own private city with the swing of a stick, the tap water he filled it with giving it a remarkably similar hue to the real thing, before it was sucked into the soil.

He was nonchalant about the river because he was perplexed by it. On the few occasions he'd seen it, he could never make out which way it flowed. Sometimes it looked to be heading west, and other times east. Once, it appeared to be flowing in both directions simultaneously. He didn't trust a river like this. And it was not a river that offered you bearings. It was so peripatetic it gave you no precise sense of place, no fixed location. It writhed and slithered with such drama it was disorienting. On purpose, the boy thought. It was a river that wanted you to be lost. He would become lost on it, and fear for his life, but that adventure was a few years away yet. And there was, too, the curious story of his great-grandmother who had drowned in the city in the 1950s, though it was something so on the periphery of his perception, not heard, exactly, but cobbled together from whispers as meagre as spider web, that it might have been something he'd made up.

Under the house, the boy never bothered recreating the bay, because who ever bothered with the bay? It could have been myth for all he knew, some prehistoric slew of mud and islands that existed just off the page of a storybook or an explorer's map – that place of sea creatures and shadowy animal–humans that came alive when you closed your eyes.

He marked the houses of both sets of grandparents with paddle-pop sticks. He signposted his own home, the little wooden colonial, with a piece of pink granite he had unearthed in the backyard. He built the low hills of Mount Coot-tha with cupped handfuls of loose soil, and with various lengths of splintery fruit-crate wood he erected the four television towers. He forested some of the city's outer suburbs with small snapped-off gum leaf clusters, attended by a handful of gritty plastic cows and horses. He didn't touch the city's mysterious frontier, a place of insect hieroglyphics in the soil, of forgotten bricks, balls of dust and hair, possum droppings and bobby pins that had fallen through the cracks between the floorboards of the house.

Purveying his replica, he might hear from upstairs heavy footfall heading down the hallway of the house, and the imaginary shopkeepers and bank clerks and office workers and pedestrians out and about in his city might dash for cover at the approach of thunder. Music from his mother's big black piano in the front room would drift down and anoint his metropolis with a festive holiday air and have its inhabitants whistling at the tram stops. And when laughter rained through the wooden floorboards from the walnut cabinet television set, everyone in the boy's town smiled because winter was almost over, or the state cricket team had won an important match, or it was a Friday, and all the way home men thought of bottles of Dinner Ale frosty in their refrigerators.

At night, in his small room at the rear of the house, he thought of his city. He loved this little room, with his desk and its bulb light and tiny globe of the world; and the navy camphor box with his favourite rocks and fool's gold fragments inside; and his plastic Viking; and his series of small war adventure books. He loved how he could open his curtains and see in the distance the blinking red light on one of the television towers. He thought it was somehow associated with the eternal light of the Sacred Heart on the altar of the church at school. He was not fond of the heavy wardrobe at the foot of his bed, for on several occasions he had woken in the night to see one of its doors wide open, and standing in the doorway a shadowed man in a felt hat, his face black and infinite. He had once screamed at the sight of the Dark Man, but no sound came out of his mouth.

The idea of his city downstairs always made him happy. What were its citizens doing now? There'd be some at the movies, and others hopping on and off the trams with their intermittent showers of blue sparks from the web of wires that hovered overhead, and other people in cars zooming past the memorial to the explorer who found the city site, and others walking up the hill past the old convict windmill or daring to enter the botanical gardens with its creaking hoop pines and the great fleshy wings of its fig trees, and others having coffee in the warm cafes near city hall, and maybe others touching the cold bronze of the lions' noses and tails in the square. His grandmother would be boiling that battered little sing-song kettle of hers for a cup of tea before bed, and across town his grandfather might be finishing one of those potboilers he liked, their covers bright with long-legged women showing a hint of brassiere, in the recliner rocker on the front veranda. Possums would be silently stepping onto chilly corrugated-iron rooves. Brush turkeys would be lurking through backyards like the ghosts of children. Men would be sitting at their workbenches downstairs, their boots covered in wood shavings, having a last cigarette for the evening. Young women, their lipstick red and fresh, would be poised in large window bays waiting to be asked for a dance in the cloud-shaped hall on the hill. And the river would be flowing backwards and forwards in the dark.

The boy knew this city of his, just as children

are aware of every rock and tree and flower in their home garden; every ant nest, toad hideaway, and foreign paw print in the exposed earth; the sound of every door, the tone of a latch, the whistle of a water pipe in their house. In his mind he had pieced the place together from stories he had heard from his parents and his grandparents, pictures he'd seen in the newspaper, and the grey images of his city on the television. Though he had never physically explored all of it, he knew it.

He had been born here. This was his home. Brisbane.

I have known it all my life – the large, dull, rectangular granite obelisk that marks the exact location where explorer and New South Wales Surveyor-General of Lands, John Oxley, set foot on the northern bank of the Brisbane River in 1824 and proclaimed a settlement site. This was the white birthplace of my city, the Caucasian holy ground, and although I had never actually stood before the obelisk, it had always been there for me, somehow, like an unremarkable freckle on the body.

In sharper relief in the mind's eye is Oxley himself, just in his early 30s and a devout Christian. His black-and-white profile — a miniature portrait rendered by an artist unknown — is as familiar to generations of Brisbane children as the A-flat of the city hall clock chimes, or the feel of summer bitumen heat through the soles of school shoes.

Oxley, it seems, wasn't a popular subject for colonial artists. That one image of him I remember from textbooks in the 1960s remains the perpetual reproduction. In the picture he appears almost boyish with his full bottom lip and helmet of pitch-black hair, tufted up in a lick above his forehead. He has a long, thinning sideburn on the left side of his face that hints at a lad straining towards manhood. His left eye looks both sleepy and watchful. Overall, though, he appears to be a good boy. It's nice, to have a good boy as the father of your hometown.

As for the obelisk, it is possibly the most unimaginative foundation stone of any city in the western world, a great 2.5-metre-high lump of grey rock, lazily chiselled and almost entirely featureless. Its back is turned to the river, its front to the North Quay sector of the CBD. Aesthetically, the obelisk says little more than 'X marks the spot', a cross in a forgotten children's fairy story. Screwed into the rock is a plaque that reads: *Here John Oxley Landing to Look for Water Discovered the Site of this City. 28th September 1824.*

The idea for the obelisk was conceived in 1924 as part of the official Brisbane Centenary celebrations – a moment, according to local chroniclers, temporarily flush with civic pride and affection for the past. It was purchased with leftover money from a state government fund set up for the Oxley commemorations.

A beautifully produced book to mark the occasion – the *Brisbane Centenary Official Historical Souvenir* – opens with an epic poem commissioned for the party. 'The Brisbane River – Oxley's Coming, 1823' was written by local laureate Emily Bulcock (sister of novelist Vance Palmer), who penned much commemorative rhyming verse in the 1920s and '30s. Curiously, the work elucidates Oxley's first journey up the river in 1823, rather than his second visit the following year that consolidated the site of the future city. Still, it gives Bulcock the opportunity to exploit the *frisson* of first contact, to *see* Brisbane – this Eden – through foreign eyes, and her lyrical narrative swings between the plunder of Paradise and the glory of a built civilisation.

Our lovely stream has fired no poet's song;
And though long centuries have seen her flow
Her age old past to silence doth belong
Ere Oxley came a hundred years ago.

Bulcock writes of the 'great white chief' seeking a stream, storming 'this Arcady' and spoiling 'the dream'. When Oxley arrives, 'the wild bird of Freedom fled away'. Then, suddenly, there is 'a sweet young city laughing in the sun'.

And round her, as around Jerusalem,
The circle of the mountains God has set;
Wherein she sparkles, a half-polished gem,
We scarce have wakened to her beauty yet.

Inside the commemorative souvenir is a further account of Oxley's second journey and the discovery of the settlement site. It notes that Oxley visited the future location of Customs House; however, 'the first centre of activity ... was a little further up the river, and it was close to the position of the Victoria Bridge [near North Quay] – there the chief buildings of the settlement soon began to arise.'

It goes on to congratulate Oxley for his site choice. 'The river has everything to do with the enduring permanence, growth and prosperity of the city, and it would be a bold man who would deny the prescience, or was it fate, which led Oxley, on his second choice, to fix upon the peninsula which is Brisbane.'

And in the 1924 book – perhaps inspired by Ms Bulcock's effusiveness – there is wild poetic flourish in the prose. 'The river always was, and is, a thing of beauty and a joy; one could almost wish that we were pagans, so that we might, as the Romans did, erect statues in appreciation of our river God.'

Jerusalem. The Romans. River gods. The great classical allusions hardly match the stolid lump of surviving granite in Oxley's name. In those days of shovel-nosed trams and fewer cars in the Roaring '20s and Depression '30s, the obelisk quite possibly attracted the historically curious with its little skirt of low cast-iron fencing. Frank Hurley, the legendary photographer–explorer–mythologiser, seemed to find it worthy of his lens. In his restless meanderings across the country after the Second World War, when he produced endless postcards and souvenir booklets for the major capital cities of Australia, he snapped a well-dressed young couple before the obelisk, standing stiffly and reading the plaque in the early afternoon. They look attired for the theatre, he in his baggy suit, and she in long skirt, mohair short-sleeved top and headscarf.

One recent winter day I, too, decide to stand on the exact location where Oxley scrambled ashore and founded Brisbane. To get to the obelisk, you must head up Makeston Street from Roma Street until you strike the T-junction with one of the city's busiest peak-hour thoroughfares – also called North Quay. Here, several lanes of traffic feed in from Coronation Drive and Hale Street in the west and funnel vehicles either into the CBD or onto the Riverside Expressway heading south. For pedestrians, it is a dead zone of sterile apartment buildings and a police credit union. There is little human traffic here, for the stretch of bitumen fronting the obelisk has been left stranded by the expressway. It is one of those eerie corners of a city that feels to have died.

The obelisk itself is half-hidden under a stand of pollution-filthy trees and hemmed in by a steel safety barrier.

Here John Oxley Landing to Look for Water Discovered the Site of this City. What are we to make of this simple, unpunctuated sentence? To a schoolboy it would present as straightforward and logical. But today it seems worded to suggest that the discovery was somehow accidental. That young Oxley stumbled upon the settlement site. He lands, looking for water, before discovering. It makes the discovery sound incidental. A surprise. Not a decision from a visionary, however wet behind the ears.

And there is something else about the iron-forged declaration. The wording seems clumsy, unconfident. There is a tremor of hesitancy about it. Perhaps it's just the absence of the commas. Perhaps it's the supposition of the memorial-plaque author to be in Oxley's head, a century after the explorer, with water at the forefront of the surveyor-general's mind. Water was a priority, but weren't there other considerations — geography, river access, timber, Indigenous inhabitants? Perhaps the author — a public servant, a member of the local historical society — was under duress, constrained to work within the small parameter of the plaque. Still, something doesn't feel right about it.

At the rear of the dreary granite block is an old brick pipe outlet, and from it pushes a steady stream of water down to a small inlet of large rocks and river mud. From the city's riverside bicycle and running track it is possible to look up, after decent rainfall, and see water cascade from this outlet. Was there once a natural watercourse here, seconded by the drain? Was it this, a clearly visible stream of fresh water, which lured Oxley to shore? The geography of landfall here would barely have changed since 1824. While the elevated Riverside Expressway may have steered traffic around the CBD, it has had a dual effect of rendering the riverbank below a no man's land, a time warp, a slice of Brisbane city topography almost prehistoric with its small-eared mangroves and silty mud.

The rocks below the obelisk are black with moisture. The bank is steep. Significantly steep, compared to the banks further south and north. Once at the top of that high ridge what would Oxley have seen? The dense rainforests across the reach of the river at West End with their wild orchids and staghorns? The low ranges and Mount Coot-tha to the west? A heavily wooded expanse of bush that sloped northward, towards the site of the future city hall which was a bog, a marsh, a dish of sponged earth teeming with frogs and insects and wild ducks?

Brisbane's journey really began in Britain in 1817 when the Third Earl Bathurst, Secretary of State for War and the Colonies, decided to hold a full commission of inquiry into the transportation of felons to New South Wales. Lord Bathurst was worried – had transportation lost its ability to punish, deter and reform criminals? And had New South Wales and other settlements outgrown their original function, to strike terror into the criminal element? In September 1819, lawyer and aristocrat John Thomas Bigge arrived in Australia to begin his investigations.

Bigge concluded that the penal system was failing as a deterrent in some instances, and recommended the establishment of new settlements to house the more recalcitrant convicts, including Moreton Bay. Bigge knew little of the bay itself, just what he had gleaned from Captain James Cook's observations and Matthew Flinders' investigations of the bay islands.

In 1822 Lord Bathurst ordered that Bigge's recommendations be carried out, and Surveyor-General John Oxley was appointed to survey the likely settlement sites. Oxley on board the *Mermaid* entered Moreton Bay on November 29, 1823, and discovered the Brisbane River. His reports excited New South Wales Governor Sir Thomas Brisbane.

The following year Oxley returned to Moreton Bay with the settlement's founding party – a total of 54 people – on board the *Amity*. He and botanist Allan Cunningham explored the river further, as the settlement was temporarily established at Redcliffe.

He had come, first and foremost, for water to sustain a military garrison. This was not a mission that considered the visual splendour and practicalities of a modern city. This was about punishment, about criminals of the Empire understanding that while Botany Bay might have gone soft on thieves and murderers, there was still somewhere in the colonies that took human corruption very seriously. Moreton Bay, as an idea, had come all the way from London. So the place was born of practicality, of the needs of immediate function and survival. Here, landing to look for permanent water, they stumbled upon the site of a future city, sank pegs into the earth, built government stores, a windmill that doubled as corn grinder and convict torturer, a prison.

I take some photographs of the obelisk, just like Hurley. I imagine Oxley clambering up those moist banks, through sharp walls of vine in his leather shoes, in his velveteen jacket, his hat off, his side levers beaded with sweat on that steamy spring afternoon.

And still the wording and location of this obelisk trouble me. In Brisbane, you don't have occasion to read many monument plaques. We have bronze statues of footballers. We have a space needle owned by a hairdressing entrepreneur, throwing eerie blue laser beams of light across the river each evening. We have street effigies of swagmen boiling billycans, left over from the World Exposition of 1988. We have electrical power boxes covered in amateur portraits of a former premier or stick figures or childish coloured patterns. The actual history of the city though is, by and large, a nameless jigsaw, a book without an index.

So I turn to the works of prominent local historian, John Steele. In his 1972 book, *The Explorers of the Moreton Bay District 1770–1830*, he reproduces extensive extracts from Oxley's Field Books regarding his journey up the Brisbane River in 1824. Oxley writes in his entry for Tuesday, September 28, the date on our city's obelisk: '... and we proceeded down the river, landing, about three-quarters of a mile from our sleeping place, to look for water, which we found in abundance and of excellent quality, being at this season a chain of ponds watering a fine valley. The soil good, with timber and a few Pines, by no means an ineligible station for a first settlement up the river.' Then Oxley sailed his government cutter to the mouth of the river where it flushed into Moreton Bay.

In his footnote attached to the word 'landing', Steele writes, 'probably at Frew Park, Milton. See Truman, *op.cit.*'

What does he mean, Frew Park, Milton? Frew Park today is a derelict, empty inner-city plot of land, the former home of the Milton Tennis Centre that was purchased in 1915 by 'Daddy Frew', the long-time president of the Queensland Lawn Tennis Association. By 1999 Tennis Queensland, crippled with debt, had sold the centre to a developer. For months the abandoned tennis courts and wooden stadium became home to vagrants. In April the following year it was torched by a 14-year-old schoolboy. The development never eventuated. Frew Park is a kilometre up the river from the obelisk at North Quay. *Landing.* The word used on the plaque attached to the obelisk. At Frew Park? And who is Truman?

There is an earlier reference to Truman in a section of the book examining the choice of the site of Brisbane. While Oxley favoured Breakfast Creek as the settlement site (later rejecting it for the quality of the fresh water and strife with local Aborigines), he was also partial — according to those Field Books — to the 'chain of ponds watering a fine valley'. T.C. Truman, the passage reveals, 'convincingly argued' in a series of articles published in Brisbane's *Courier-Mail* in 1950 that the site of the 'chain of ponds' was in fact at Milton, an old riverside suburb and home to the famous XXXX brewery in the city's inner-west. 'The incident has sometimes been construed as the discovery of the site of Brisbane,' writes Steele.

So if the discovery of the site of Brisbane was at Milton, what is the obelisk doing at North Quay?

Retrieving the *Courier-Mail* articles from the newspaper's microfiche library, I learn that Tom Truman was an academic in the Department of History at the University of Queensland — itself just a little further up the river from Milton, and a place Oxley's party camped one evening while exploring the river.

The headline for the first part of Truman's series, published on Saturday, April 29, 1950, is 'Rewriting the History of the Birth of Brisbane'. The newspaper is hardly shying away from something momentous here, a revelation, a historic bombshell overlooked for more than 126 years since the conception of the city. 'The general history of the settlement is well known but there have always been gaps in the story', the newspaper says in a break-out box explaining the Truman series.

Truman himself opens with: 'Things and places that are part of our daily lives and have become tedious through their familiarity, can take on a new interest for us if we know their history.' Could he be alluding to the dreary obelisk, described by Catholic Archbishop James Duhig, in a speech to a Brisbane Rotary Club in March 1934, as the 'not imposing' cairn on the spot where Oxley *was said* to have landed?

It is not until part three of the serial, published the following Saturday, that Truman rolls out his hand grenade. Could Oxley have actually landed at Milton, and not at North Quay, where the memorial still stands?

Truman spends much of the article reproducing quotes from Oxley's Field Books, then comes to that crucial entry for September 28: '... and we proceeded down the river, landing, about three-quarters of a mile from our sleeping place, to look for water, which we found in abundance and of excellent quality, being at this season a chain of ponds watering a fine valley.' Truman ponders:

'These words constitute for Brisbane what Batman's "This is the spot for a village" is to Melbourne. On this evidence the site for the Oxley memorial on North Quay was fixed. This decision may well have been correct, but doubts Oxley's actual landing place "about three-quarters of a mile from our sleeping place".'

For Truman's hypothesis to be true – that Oxley's genuine landing spot was further west up the river than the obelisk – he had to prove the location of Oxley's 'sleeping place' on the night of Monday, September 27. In the Field Book entry for that day, Oxley says his party encountered a large tribe of Aborigines on the banks of the river, at the present-day suburb of Toowong, according to Truman, westward of Milton, and decided to pitch camp 'about half-mile below this encampment on the same side of the river there being a small creek between us, which I hoped would prevent them visiting us'. This would put the camp at the present-day Patrick Lane, Toowong, near the Wesley Hospital. The next morning, in search of fresh water, Oxley's party 'landed about three-quarters of a mile from our sleeping place'. This, according to Truman, would fix Oxley's actual landing spot and discovery of the city site where the old

Western Creek entered the river below Coronation Drive in Milton. The distance from Patrick Lane to the memorial at North Quay is, as the article notes, over 'one and a half miles'. How could an experienced navigator like Oxley get his distance so wrong?

'One assumes that the men who fixed the site for the memorial must have had additional data. I should very much like to know what that extra information was', crows a triumphant Truman.

In 1988 (and amidst another historic flush, this time the bicentennial of Australia, with a nod to the tourism influx expected for Expo), 38 years after Truman made his revelations, and 16 years after Steele repeated them in his book *The Explorers of the Moreton Bay District*, a memorial to Oxley at the actual site in Milton was unveiled by the then Lord Mayor of Brisbane, Sallyanne Atkinson. Situated inside the atrium of a pedestrian twin-towered business building called 'Oxley Centre', it consists of three glass and steel posts that look like the ragged remnants of a ship's sail. Inscribed into the glass are extracts from the Field Books. At the base of the memorial is parked a busy coffee cart, attended each weekday morning by a queue of office workers.

Across Coronation Drive and opposite the Oxley Centre is another plaque, also unveiled in 1988, commemorating Oxley's epochal landing 'hereabouts'. It is positioned in a neat little culvert beside a bus stop.

At the point where the old Western Creek now emerges into the Brisbane River, there is the city's only over-the-water restaurant unambiguously called 'Oxley's On the River'. It serves Moreton Bay bugs, sand crab frittata and 'Oxley's fish and chips'.

To the right of the restaurant is a set of small concrete steps that lead down to the river's edge a short distance from the creek outlet, which is now a wide concreted canal. On the steps is an old canned-fruit tin for the cigarette butts of the restaurant's chefs and waiting staff. Was this, the old Western Creek, the source of water Oxley first noted and which lured him to shore, to landing, looking for water, and to the beautiful chain of ponds watering a fine valley?

I contact Reverend Steele about the historical anomalies, the obelisk at North Quay, and the apparent lack of care, or interest, in celebrating the city's actual birthplace.

'Many years ago someone associated with the

John Oxley Library told me that the monument was an afterthought to use up funds allocated for the Centenary, and that its placement at North Quay was intended to be temporary pending a more precise identification of the site where Oxley had camped', he tells me in an email. 'Although it has long been acknowledged that North Quay is not the correct site, as far as I know no one in officialdom has taken the initiative to relocate it.'

Oxley made three trips to Brisbane in his lifetime. According to Steele, he never once set foot in the Brisbane 'pocket' or current site of the CBD. It was the first commandant at Moreton Bay – Lieutenant Henry Miller – who set up the settlement at the site fanning out from the obelisk. And Steele believes it was John Grey – the Pilot of Port Jackson, sent north from Sydney to oversee the permanent relocation of the settlement from its temporary beginnings in Redcliffe to North Quay – who decided upon the precise location for settlement. It was he, and Miller, who climbed the steep banks of the river not far from the obelisk.

The steep bank. The peninsular on which the CBD sits today. Oxley went with the water, but Miller sought geographic protection. This is precisely the theory of Brisbane historian and author of *The Brisbane River Story: Meander Through Time*, Helen Gregory.

'The question of the obelisk,' she tells me, 'is one that could occupy an all-day seminar. I think it was placed where it was simply because it was *central* to everything, and did not rely on historical accuracy. You have to remember, too, that Oxley was a Naval person. But the first commandant [Miller] was an Army man. Army people very much look towards the disposition of the land and how the settlement might be protected in the event of attack. Oxley and Miller saw the land in two very different ways.'

The revelation of the misplaced obelisk unexpectedly upsets me, as might the discovery of a crucial anomaly in the family tree. The boy in me, the boy who admired John Oxley, the boy who revelled in his town's convict history and drew, in his exercise books, tall-hatted commandants overseeing chain gangs, who always craned his neck to see the obelisk, as the family's mint-green HQ Holden station wagon heaved through North Quay, had been told a fib. The boy felt foolish.

My grandmother, Freda, travelled with her family from London to Brisbane in early 1925 aboard the S.S. Ormuz, an Orient steamship. The ship was formerly the German-made Zeppelin, seized by the United States to return troops from Europe at the end of World War I. They boarded the ship at Tilbury Docks in London, and en route the ship docked at Naples, Suez, Aden and Colombo. According to family anecdotes, when the ship approached Fremantle the family saw a giant bushfire engulfing the coastline. Freda, born in Reading, was nine years old. Her father, Albert, was a journeyman tailor. Her mother Kate once worked as a packer at the Huntley & Palmers biscuit factory in Reading. Shortly before she died in a Gold Coast Hospital in 1996, I asked my grandmother what she thought of her life in Brisbane. 'I hated it,' she said. 'I have hated every day of it since I stepped off the ship.'

Buried deep beneath the boy's suburban Brisbane house, beyond the miniature city he had built with his small hands in the cool wedge of space, past the net of grass runners and clover shoots out in the yard, further down than the buried and forgotten surveyor pegs, the subdivision developer's soiled bunting flags, the fragments of broken brick and

27

tile and the wet worms and bugs that played in the soil and, sometimes, in the boy's dreams, were granite boulders as large as dinosaur eggs.

He knew they were down there. He could feel their shapes under the soles of his bare feet when he played about the yard. In summer, especially in the early morning or just before nightfall, he sensed the cold curve of them on his high arches.

Some of them broke the surface of the backyard: smooth heads hatched to the blast-heat of February, or coated with June dew. There was a cluster of them, pale and skin-coloured – three bald men whispering to each other over by the Hills Hoist. But there were the others way down beneath the concrete stumps and septic tank and clay pipes of the house, and at night in his narrow bed, he thought of them, large and warm and shouldering each other through the dark earth.

Later, he was unable to decide if the boulders were his earliest memory, or just a recollection appropriated from a handful of old Polaroids he'd seen, taken in the mid-1960s, where the world seemed washed through with a green chemical that made the sky look dangerous and the humans poorly.

There was another memory that was maybe not

a real memory. An upside-down window frame, and through it the black leaves of a tree and silhouetted globes of fruit, seemingly defying gravity and growing upward out of the leaf hands. Before they had moved into the house of boulders, his mother told him, they had a rented a small cottage nearby. He was no more than a year old. Outside the window of the bedroom he shared with his twin sister, beyond the cots, was a sticky mango tree. Could you have such a memory? Could one-year-old eyes, just seeing the world, take such an image like a holiday postcard off a wire rack and carry it through life? He wasn't sure. He liked to think the framed picture of the mangoes was a correspondence he had mailed to himself through the years.

At the boulder house, though, he could definitely close his eyes and vividly see his father and grandfather at work in the dreary yard, not long after the wood and brick home his parents built became habitable. A young and an older man labouring around the ovoid heads of granite with wood-handled picks – two pioneers clearing a selection. Soon after, the boy became obsessed with pen-and-ink sketches of men just like them in his school history books: the convicts in their blackbird sacking, swinging hammers and pickaxes just a few kilometres away near the old windmill on Wickham Terrace; others in chains at the farm and grazing paddocks at Gardens Point on the bend of the river, or across the water at the Kangaroo Point quarry.

After scratching fresh moats around the rocks, the boy's father and grandfather then set fires in the gullies. These would burn for days. They crackled away while his dad went to work as a bank clerk in Town, a thin, diligent young finance officer labouring at a wooden desk in a building constructed of the very Brisbane Tuff that those blackbirds had carved out of the cliffs across the river.

The boy watched the little fires outside in the yard; pressed his nose against the windowglass and felt both thrilled and frightened by the primitive glowing about the shadows of rock, while inside *The Honeymooners* yabbered and fought on the huge wood-grained television set with its four angled legs, and the scent of Swipe lingered about the kitchen and the *faux* colonial wood-turned lounge chairs, and invisible chemical motes clothed his mother's precious figurines.

When the rocks had fully absorbed the fire heat, buckets of water were sluiced over their curves, and they cracked and yawned as granite had probably done since the beginning of time, till they could be extracted like crumbled teeth.

The boy had read somewhere of the great volcanic eruptions of the region, being obsessed with rocks and lava and fool's gold (he had a little amber medicine bottle containing precious granules of it, picked with a nail from the driveway of his primary school), and had seen the marvellous and creepy plugs of the Glasshouse Mountains to the north, and concluded that these eggs beneath him in suburban Brisbane had been flung a hundred kilometres south from the great gorilla of Tibrogargan, or from Beerwah or Beerburrum, more than 200 million years before. In the Space-obsessed '60s – a phantasmagoric cavalcade of pincer-handed robots, sleek rockets and mechanical child heroes capable of unleashing tremendous strength and horrible vengeance – the notion of such force, at least to the boy, was entirely real. It seemed fantastic, though, that his shirtless young father, with just a worn wood-handled pick, fire and water could, in less than a week, dislodge something so ancient.

Because of the nearby volcanoes, and the boulders, and the penny turtles in the creek down past the giant stand of bamboo at the end of the street, and the frill-necked lizards on the rocks beside the creek, and his rock collection, and the copper-coloured skinks that made their way into the house, and the scarab beetles that sometimes inched up the curtains and snagged their feet on the cotton, and myriads of other things, his childhood felt very connected with the earth and its creatures. Often, there was no division between the inside and outside of the house when it came to birds and moths and ladybirds and lizards and stick insects. They carried on their way as if the house wasn't there. There were snakes in the bushes, and plants whose sap could kill you if taken on the tongue. A pupil at school had died from the sting of a bee, and the boy had attended the funeral on the rugby oval, and stared at the polished, dark wood coffin resting on its shiny silver gurney and thought of the flowering clover beneath the rubber wheels. A possum had frozen to death one winter, clinging to the stringy-bark tree off the veranda. He had seen the death-set of its teeth and dull eyes before they put the body in a fruit crate and solemnly walked it to the end of the street where the bitumen gave way to the bush, and buried it in the long grass. There was death in this place that was teeming with life.

Each evening, deliberately parting the curtains of his bedroom at the back of the house so he could see the stars and the moon beyond the ratty eucalypts, he thought of the solid eggs beneath, and they made him feel safe. As did the sacred blinking red light of the Mount Coot-tha television tower. This was his home, and he was secure knowing what wheeled overhead at night, and what rested underneath.

His family's was a modest three-bedroom brick home on a sloping block. It was built around 1963, and presumably had risen from some stock-standard tableaux of designs favoured by a suburban developer a year or so earlier. So it borrowed more from the box-like '50s than the curved, space-aged '60s. It was what they colloquially called back then a 'colonial' home, or a box with a frilly, wrought-iron face. His family gestured to a colonial past inside the house as well, with fake kerosene lanterns and bush prints in imitation wooden frames. This was a distorted dream of early Australia; it set the family as modern pioneers on their small rectangular purchase.

The back of the house was hinged to the earth on the slope, the front supported by thin metal poles. This created the triangular wedge of space underneath the house. A carport had been gouged out of the soil to the right, beneath what was the kitchen and dining room. The remaining space, under the bedrooms and lounge room, was raw, angled earth. This was where the boy disappeared, into his city.

It was that rare place in childhood where you could vanish and remain unobserved for long periods of time. For the boy it was never threatening, no matter how much darkness gathered. The giant eggs were just a pick-axe away. And you could always hear someone moving about upstairs, a shifting weight on the thin boards, bare skin, slippers or thongs; the long, disorienting rhythm of someone walking the full length of the house down the central hallway, the staccato of the linoleum-tiled kitchen, the heavy then delicately spaced shuffling of the those entering and exiting the lavatory. He knew who was who from the different tones and what they were up to. It was the music of his family, amplified in that earthy drum of his under-the-house. It was the domestic score to the drama of his city. He could not know, yet, that there were other, greater dramas in the world, because this was all he comprehended. He had no wider reference.

Brisbane was New York, or Rome, or Paris. A city. Though where others beat with history and the tremors of the moment, his was quietly and gently shaped by the grand monotony of suburbia.

He spent a lot of time down there in his city. His mother probably thought it unnatural. What he did was of no interest to his twin sister. They might have shared the same gravity, but when she was on the dark side of the moon he was in the light, and vice versa. He had no idea how his father viewed it. His father was the man who left the breakfast nook with its star-flecked Formica table in the early morning, and came home at dusk (the familiar sound of the car engine on the driveway) five times a week at precisely the same time (scrambling loose the fabric of the day, sending the heart soaring), bringing the smell of a day's labour and the leather of a stitched briefcase held in a large hand at the level of the boy's face. It was a generational ritual for countless children. And the father at home in the evening triggered the slow rituals towards sleep. He had no concept of what his father actually thought. But he knew for a fact that his father had a tree house when he was a boy, in a backyard just a few kilometres north-east across the range, for he had seen its rotting black skeleton deep inside the sticky mango tree at the back of his grandparents' house. So his father must have had some affinity with the boy's need for private space, the attraction of it for some boys, this quiet refuge that some boys then take inside of themselves, as men.

When the boy became that man, he found it harder to get back there, to that place, to find what was such a part of him, and he of it — this city he was once so integral to that you could have observed its landscape and he would have been in there and you would not have seen him. But he was there, a little strand of Brisbane.

As a man he moved away, because as he grew bigger his city grew smaller, and he thought he needed more space, and he believed, as a lot of young people in his city believed, that he had seen all of life in Brisbane, that it had not grown with him since he was a boy, that he was shedding skin and the hills, the houses, the river, and all the landmarks of his life were exactly as they were in childhood, just a little shabbier, and uglier, and sadder. He believed he hated his city, because he had built it in the cool shade under the house when he was little and life was limitless and time moved so slowly, and now life was faster and newer but Brisbane had grown and changed so little it would still fit under that old house. He resented it because of that. He had an idea that by its very apathy his city had evicted him, kicked him out. You think you're too big for me? Then go away. I don't want you anymore.

He moved away, and the city moved away from him. Yet he always had his city inside him, and over the years it grew bigger in his mind, and as he dug back, through the grass runners, into the loose soil, deeper into the dirt and clay towards the giant warm eggs, he was stricken with what he might have described to himself as longing.

Somewhere, a long way away, he could hear a mother's sing-song voice calling children in for dinner. It's getting dark. The streetlights flicker on. Then there is the sound of the car engine in the drive. The rich smell of leather. Bathed, he still bears streaks of green grass on his knees. A blanket is pulled up to his chin. And he is in that small, perfectly remembered little childhood room, with a globe of the world next to his bedside lamp on the desk, pulling the curtains back just a little, to reveal the palette of stars.

Now, as a middle-aged man, I decide to go down to the Milton landing site and follow the line of the old creek in search of Oxley's chain of ponds. As Truman writes: 'I am told by old residents that there were chains of waterholes connected by the Western Creek which had its rise in a swamp with the picturesque name of Red Jacket Swamp which has since become Gregory Park next to the Milton State School. This creek used to flow through the areas now called Frew Park and Milton Park and came out at Dunmore Bridge, on Coronation Drive. The last part of it has been converted into a drain.'

I am quietly excited because the boy in me is discovering his city for the first time, tracing the steps of his hero Oxley, erasing the fib. With the infinite confidence of a child I am convinced I'll be able to see beyond my time, beyond the office buildings and blocks of units and bitumen roads and computer stores and tanning salons, and at the very least feel the shape of the natural landscape that the surveyor-general first stepped into. I can clearly imagine the landscape of my childhood in Brisbane, 47 years ago, and what I remember is not fantastically different from what I can see in the city today. The river hasn't moved. The hills and gullies of the inner-west haven't gone away. So why couldn't I go back less than another 150 years, and see Oxley's valley?

I begin at the old Western Creek outlet on the river, as Oxley did, and work in the reverse of Truman's description. The drain that empties into the river, near the restaurant workers' cigarette tin, runs beneath Coronation Drive and the Oxley Centre. From a walkway underneath the drive it's still possible to see wooden fragments of the old Dunmore Bridge. Once under the Oxley Centre the broad drain then passes beneath a stretch of road and railway line before it emerges again, as a canal, running along the edge of Milton Park. In historical ignorance, I have brought my young son to this park dozens of times: there is a metal children's train he enjoys clambering over.

The grubby watercourse then takes a slight dog-leg, turning to the north, and disappears beneath Milton Road and the dilapidated open field of Frew Park and the former site of the Milton Bowl bowling alley (where my mother played in a league for many years prior to its demolition) before running beneath Gregory Park (and its cricket pitch and phantasmagoria of children's swings where I have also taken my boy too many times to remember).

Gregory Park adjoins the Milton State School, where both my mother and grandfather were pupils. Grandfather and his wife, Freda, lived in nearby Beck Street. So my maternal grandparents spent most of their life a few hundred metres from the chain of ponds.

Having been born in Brisbane, I left the city in my early 20s and remained away for two decades, returning to live in a house with my own family, also just a few hundred metres from the chain of ponds. In total, my life and family history have intersected with Brisbane's birthplace for almost a century. I didn't know it. I never knew the facts.

Today I walk the modern streets laid over Oxley's landing place. I imagine the location of his campsite and the place where he jotted in his Field Book, possibly by the light of a fire, that here was a place 'by no means an ineligible station for a first settlement up the river'. I continue on foot beyond Gregory Park to the sharp ridges of Paddington, in Brisbane's inner-west, and look south towards the river and delineate, for the first time, the scoop of earth that was Oxley's 'fine valley'. I go home, a few minutes' walk away, to my house perched at the edge of a side gully of that valley. In a matter of hours, my view of the city has been altered forever.

Late in the evening, with the house and suburb well asleep, I sit out in the cold on the back deck and peer down the forested gully in the direction of the river. It is quiet except for the occasional scratch and hiss of possums through the Chinese elms and gum trees. In September of 1824 Oxley must have heard this too; the devilish guttural screech of the possums; the strange scampering of brush turkeys through the undergrowth. He must have smelled the wood smoke from the Aboriginal camps, not as sharp as his own fire, but spread and strained through the eucalypts.

I think about the obelisk. How there are two sites claiming ownership to Oxley's landing. How almost two centuries have passed and nobody has bothered to clarify the record; to set things straight. I wonder why nobody cared enough to do that.

I recall how historical landmarks in this city have often been demolished on quiet nights just like this – the Bellevue Hotel, Cloudland – and yet they left the obelisk. *Here John Oxley Landing to Look for Water Discovered the Site of this City.* Here, an outpost for recalcitrant convicts. Here, a penal colony built to take the pressure off another, more powerful, more robust settlement. A secondary place. Something that germinated out of a government order, not from those human wellsprings of hope, endeavour, courage. A harsh, hot tableau of public servants in their woollen uniforms and high boots designed for an English climate, out to please southern masters. A town for the sharp talk of spivs and murderers; a violent place built on deception and aggression; and with them the entrepreneurs feeding off this government project. And at the top of Queen Street – not far from the present-day Executive Building and seat of state government – was erected the huge wooden A-frame where early transgressors were publicly flogged. Government and citizen. Cruelty and fear. Fact and fiction.

I thought I knew my city. What else is there I don't know? Then I have a thought that brings the cold of the night into my stomach. I also know absolutely nothing of my own family's history in this place, beyond two sets of grandparents. And even their stories are unclear, fuzzy at the edges with the omissions, diversions, false scents and often out-and-out obstructions offered by surviving family members over the decades. Have I shared the same collective Brisbane mindset that couldn't be bothered addressing the truth of the Oxley monument? Is this what we are like here?

I remember something Brisbane-born author David Malouf once wrote about this place in his essay 'A First Place: The Mapping of a World'. He discusses the city's topography — 'walk two hundred metres in almost any direction outside the central city and you get a view — a new view. It is all gullies and sudden vistas.' He then writes: 'Wherever the eye turns here it learns restlessness, and variety and possibility, as the body learns effort. Brisbane is a city that tires the legs and demands a certain sort of breath. It is not a city, I would want to say, that provokes contemplation, in which the mind moves out and loses itself in space. What it might provoke is drama, and a kind of intellectual play, delights in new and shifting views, and this because each new vista as it presents itself here is so intensely colourful.'

I understand, shockingly, at this moment on the back deck, that I have lived with some form of historical amnesia. That I have not *contemplated*; that I am, in truth, disconnected from the place where I came into the world, when I always thought I was a part of its fabric, that it was essential to who I am.

Here, on this night, I think of the obelisk over beside the expressway, the granite dark and gathering dew on its river side, the words *John Oxley* on the plaque sporadically illuminated by vehicle brakelights where it faces the traffic, and wonder why my city of Brisbane grew up on a lie.

Embedded on the sidewalk in Albert Street, the city, as part of the Writers' Walk, is a circular brass plaque that depicts the first verse of a poem by local writer David Rowbotham. The poem is titled 'Brisbane' (1971), and the verse is a devastating salvo to the city. 'Born in 1824, by rape', it opens, and goes on to decry its citizens for a pedigree of abjection to authority. 'It still repeats the meek and musket age', the verse ends. The rest of the poem is equally direct. 'Worn-timid town assuming hometown progress', it says, 'in every history-book an outpost, or pageless...' I decide to telephone Rowbotham, who is 84 and lives quietly in Holland Park.

'The city was a compound, a prison without a wall,' he says in a voice still crisp at the edges with that British correctness of the middle of last century. 'We had the cat-o'-nine-tails, the triangle, slavery ... it was a hard place, and it was a hard place to live in, even for me. "It still repeats

*the meek and musket age." Yes, that's Brisbane, Queensland.
Still subservient to the powers that be.'*

On March 2, 1926, a full eighteen months after the
celebrations had come and gone, newly installed
Mayor William Jolly received a curious memo from
his City Treasurer's Department. It stated: 'At a
meeting of the Trustees of the Centenary Celebrations Fund… it was resolved that you, as Mayor of
Brisbane, be asked if you would make arrangements
for the supply of granite block and the erection
of same on North Quay, under the supervision of
the Town Planner and Dr Cumbrae-Stewart. This
granite block will bear a tablet suitably inscribed,
and will serve to commemorate the landing of
Oxley at North Quay… Dr Cumbrae-Stewart is
undertaking to arrange for the supply of the tablet
and the inscription thereon.'

With this began a storm that would last more
than a decade, and involve bitter disputes and personality clashes among Brisbane's academic elite –
and expose connections that would reach as high
as Government House, the beautiful but quixotic
'Fernberg' in inner-city Paddington.

As for that memo to the mayor in 1926, the incorrect siting of the obelisk was apparently already in train, and the author was, it appears, the respected Dr F.W.S. Cumbrae-Stewart, co-founder of the state's historical society and keeper of its factual bedrock, president of the Brisbane Dickens Fellowship, vice-president of the Queensland Authors' and Artists' Association, and newly appointed Garrick Professor of Law at the young University of Queensland. His inaugural lecture as Professor would be 'The Law and the City'.

It was Cumbrae-Stewart who soon took the obelisk under his wing. It would be Cumbrae-Stewart who made sure it was put at North Quay. It was he who wrote – *Here John Oxley Landing to Look for Water Discovered the Site of this City. 28th September 1824.*

Who was he? And how could a man described by the Brisbane *Courier-Mail* as 'a human encyclopaedia on matters pertaining to the history of this State', have gotten his facts so wrong?

As I look at these documents at the Brisbane City Council Archives, Annabel Lloyd, Archives Co-ordinator, says to me, 'So many people contact us wanting to know about the real history of Brisbane,' she said. 'But there's hardly anything. It's hard to know where to point them to.' The book without an index.

Afterwards I think about F.W.S. Cumbrae Stewart. Sometimes hyphenated in the records, sometimes not. Cumbrae-Stewart. It, too, doesn't sound right. It is clumsy and ill-fitting, like the wording on the monument.

I need to find out who this man with the strange surname was — so integral, it seems, to the keeping of records in this city, indeed the father of some of our major historical repositories, and, by proxy, an early architect of our future past.

One evening I sit at the dinner table with my son who is almost four and has green grass stains on his trousers and the elbows of his jumper, and he exudes the odour of warm grass. The louvers face our street, and we're not far from my late grandmother's house in Rosalie. A streetlight outside flickers on and its white balloon is wobbly-edged against the glass — and it all goes around again: I am there and I am here, and I can do this in Brisbane because unlike the great seething, rejuvenating, reincarnating cities of the world, time here seems to move slower, and the distance from founding to present is less. It continues to intersect. In a place with few historical reminders, it does this in your heart. Somehow, in Brisbane, the past is just beyond the windowsill.

My son is, like so many boys his age, obsessed with dinosaurs. Inside a Tupperware container beside his bed, we have one hatching from a soft-ball-sized egg submerged in water. Each morning he wakes excitedly to see the magnitude of the cracks, and what may be nestling inside the pale pink shell. There are a dozen plastic Diplodo-cus and Icthyosaurus and Triceratops sharing his murky fishtank with a handful of guppies and a furry deep-sea diver. I think of Brisbane's past as a small, coiled dinosaur skeleton – not a giant Diplodocus but perhaps a nimble Gallimimus – its ribs and vertebrae, its *infrastructure*, all tight and within touching distance of each other in a raw bed of earth. And I think the past here is within touching distance, but so is life. In Brisbane, the head always seems to know what the tail is doing. This is a place of unending coincidences. In a city of about 2 million people, everybody seems to know your business. Either that, or the lines of communication are more streamlined, the distance between the ribs and the vertebrae much less than in other major cities. A columnist for the *Moreton Bay Courier* wrote in March 1859 of hearing one gentleman ask another, 'How is it the people of Moreton Bay appear to pay more attention to other people's business than their own?'

I look down at my son, he with the same thick, tawny, tousled hair I had as a boy. Is it another Brisbane disposition, this melancholy for the past, this obsession with the passage of time, and the strangely sentimental, almost medieval, view of life in a seasonal way, in a subtropical place that disregards the clock of traditional seasons? It has all come full circle, I think, looking at my boy. I begin to sense, as you might see the after-image of a fork of lightning across the sky, the ghostly blue outlines of ancient eggs.

I ask him what he did with his day. He tells me he went to preschool (over near the old Lang Park, and both upon the site of Brisbane's first major city cemetery). Then he invited a friend home, and they played together in the backyard.

'What did you play?' I ask him.

'We built a city,' he tells me.

'What with?'

'With rocks and sticks and leaves.'

'Which city?' I ask.

'Brisbane,' he says.

It's very still outside and the air has that abrupt tautness it gets here before an electrical storm, an animal frozen at the twig crack of a predator, everything unmoving.

In that instant before the deluge, with my boy beside me at the dining table, in the bulb light that becomes intensely yellow as the world grows suddenly dark outside, and still comprehending the news that he, too, has built his own replica of Brisbane, I hear something that constricts my throat. Having wafted around office buildings, across the railway yards at Roma Street, up Petrie Terrace, down the ridge, over an uneven plate of corrugated-iron rooves, through the coin leaves of the Chinese elm in our backyard and into the dining room, the A-flat chime of the city hall clock arrives at our table.

One early summer day in 1982, when I was waiting in my car at the set of traffic lights at the T-junction of Sylvan Road and Coronation Drive in Toowong, I travelled back in time.

I was the first car at the lights, and through the windscreen I could see the fig trees straight ahead, and beyond them the brown Brisbane River. As the traffic on Coronation Drive blurred past, I found myself staring at the tree canopies, and for a moment the many thousands of green waxen leaves shivered together in the breeze.

The sensation, for a fraction of a second, was that I had been transported back to Brisbane before European settlement, and that it was very quiet, and the figs with their lovely winged roots and dense canopies were here then on this bend of the river, laying out their shade towards the water.

The light of the place was still brutal, fierce in the middle of the day – then and now – and could have been nowhere else but Brisbane. Was it the light at that precise moment, in concert with the movement of the fig leaves, a stupefying heat pressing against the glass and metal of the vehicle, and sentiment perhaps thrumming through me after the visit to my grandmother at her timber house near the chain of ponds, that made me think I had gone back a couple of centuries? Was it something about this patch of earth beside the river, a five-minute walk from where Oxley came ashore in 1824? Was it just a product of imagination, or an illusion?

For years since I have passed that spot facing Coronation Drive and remembered the moment, mulled over it, tried to understand it. As a boy I had been obsessed with the film *The Time Machine* starring Rod Taylor, and the little whirring device with its plush red seat that sent a cigar, and ultimately Taylor's character H. George Wells, many centuries into the future. This fascination stayed with me through childhood.

Why didn't it leave me? And why did I never think of time-travelling into the future, only into the past? Why did I feel a need to go back, over and over, and what was I looking for? The insistence of this idea suggested to me, later in life, that my childhood must have had questions that were never answered, gaps in the continuum, hidden spaces, blind corridors. Our family narrative did have plot flaws, details glossed over and a crooked logic. Was this just the nature of families, the unmentioned as powerful and real as the declared? Did Brisbane have anything to do with this?

I keep coming back to the light of Brisbane. If you are born into it, this palette of gentle pinks and oranges at dawn and dusk, the blast white of midday in summer, the lemon luminescence of mid-morning and mid-afternoon, you keep it with you, and measure all other light by it. If you live away from it, then step back into it, it is the first thing that tells you you're home. You might find other places that come close to it – the Mediterranean, for example – but nothing seems to replicate its vibrancy, nor its converse delicacy.

It can be violently vivid in the belly of storm clouds, or as gentle as a blush at first light, coming over the city quietly so as not to stir its people. It's a light that can produce, at the right time of day, very black and very hard-edged shadows. It's a light so raw it can put everyone in the city onstage. At the apex of its whiteness, it can bleach out people and buildings and throw everything into a shapeless mirage. It can frighten you or put a smile on your face. It's an overwhelming sort of light that elicits grand questions in you, then just as quickly pins your insignificant self firmly to the earth. Sometimes, depending on the season and the clouds, it can illuminate the city as a small warm lamp may light a room. It can be moody, unpredictable, beautiful and ugly, and its ability to shift and awe is what makes it a constant in your life if you were born into it.

Brisbane architect Robin Gibson, who designed the Queensland Cultural Centre precinct on the river at South Bank, said of his art gallery's skylights in a lecture in 1980, 'Warmly bathing this water mall zone [in the yet to be constructed gallery] will be the same beautiful daylight which so many of our artists and sculptors have captured... the same quality of daylight which revealed itself through the tents of the early inhabitants in 1825 – the same revealing daylight which penetrated the verandas and articulated the facades of the architectural beauties of the past – a quality of light which cannot be destroyed – a light which demands reverence – a light of joy.'

In David Malouf's short story, 'Dream Stuff', the lead character, Colin, a Brisbane expatriate, returns to the city after many years and it is the constancy of the light that gives him a connection to his past life. 'He had long understood that one of his selves, the earliest and most vulnerable, had never left this place, and that his original and clearest view of things could be recovered only through what had first come to him in the glow of its ordinary light and weather. In a fig tree taller than a building and alive with voices not its own, or a line of palings with a gap you could crawl through into a wilderness of nut-grass and cosmos and saw-legged grasshoppers as big as wrens.

'It was the light they appeared in that was the point, and that at least had not changed. It fell on the new city with the same promise of an ordinary grace as on the old. He greeted it with the delight of recovery, not only of the vision but of himself.'

Is Colin time-travelling via the Brisbane light? Is this what happened to me at that T-junction when I was a young man? What is it about Brisbane and time?

For decades after first settlement the city had an awkward relationship with time. In 1857 the town of close to 6000 was excited by the enterprise of local shopkeepers J. & G. Harris, who announced they were erecting an imported London 'turret' clock at their store. They promised the clock bells would be heard for two miles. The *Moreton Bay Courier* applauded Messrs Harris, saying the clock would 'supply a want which has long been felt'. The local paper made no further mention of the promised clock.

And four years later a time-ball was proposed for the old convict windmill on Wickham Terrace. The ball would drop at 1pm each day. In April 1866, the member for North Brisbane, former journalist and publisher, Theophilus Pugh, asked the colonial secretary in parliament when the government might provide a time-gun for the windmill (then called the 'Brisbane Observatory'), in lieu of the time-ball. He was told arrangements were being made.

The time-gun proved to be a public nuisance and a cause for perennial debate. Anti-time-gun letters peppered the *Courier*, along with pleadings for a striking clock. By the 1870s the city had a few time indicators, but none that were reliable, thus aggravating citizens, keeping them permanently beyond the consolatory precision of mother's beating heart in Greenwich.

'There is one very great want in our rapidly increasing city which is considerably felt by every citizen in Brisbane', said a letter in the *Courier* in March 1876. 'What I refer to is, *one and the correct time*. At present we have the time-gun, the Post Office and Railway clocks, to refer to – three distinct times – and on Saturday last… there was a difference of five minutes between the first and the last of them. Which was right? Which was wrong? How are we possibly to regulate our watches and timepieces? are questions frequently asked and impossible to be answered.' The following year,

another resident wrote: 'The want of a good striking clock in Brisbane is generally acknowledged; for
besides that belonging to the Post Office, which
during the bustle of Queen-street traffic, cannot be
heard a hundred yards, there is no other.'

Yet by the 1880s the time-gun was still boom-
ing away, rattling the crockery and rocking the
house stumps of Brisbane. 'As it is at present the
report is a nuisance', wrote in an incensed local,
signed A. SUFFERER, 'shaking houses so as to damage their structure, frightening horses, and especially disturbing any person who is ill. In the houses
near windows have to be kept open in all weathers
to prevent their being broken by the concussion.
Surely, sir, in these days when a good timekeeper
can be purchased for a few shillings, such a practice
is a remnant of barbarism.'

Another debate flared about its location. 'I
differ altogether with your correspondent who
wants to have the time-gun fired from the top of
Mount Coot-tha. The sound would be dissipated
at once, and, in many states of the wind, would
be heard only in the gum trees. The proper place
for the time-gun would be on the river bank, in
the Government Gardens, with its muzzle pointed
straight at the highest part of the perpendicular

rocks on… Kangaroo Point. The sound would, from these rocks, be reverberated all over the city and suburbs…'

It wasn't until January 1, 1895 – seventy years after the first settlement at North Quay – that the Standard Time Act came into operation, determining 'one time' for the entire colony, 'uniform with the mean time of the 150th meridian east of Greenwich, or exactly ten hours earlier than Greenwich time.' The time-ball was finally brought into full operation again in the old windmill in preparation for the passing of the Time Bill. But it was 1930 before the time could be seen and heard for a certainty.

Only then, it seems, did the people of Brisbane live their lives in synchronicity with the rest of the world, with the arrival of the clock in the Brisbane city hall tower. It was made by the Synchronome Electrical Company of Australia and its proprietor Albert George Jackson, of Ann Street, Brisbane. Designed and installed by his son, Arthur Appleton Jackson, the clock had been commissioned in 1927 for the opening of city hall in 1930.

The four plain dials weigh more than three tons, and contain one ton of white opal. The clock-face glass is held by over 1000 screws. The hour hands are almost six feet long. The minute hands are ten feet long. Inside the old cage-lift within the clock tower, as you ascend towards the small, cramped viewing platform at the top of the tower, you pass through a gentle block of pale yellow light diffused through the opal faces.

The clock is controlled by a master pendulum, a duplicate of the Slave Clock at the entrance to the Royal Observatory at Greenwich – the first clock to show Greenwich Mean Time to the public. The Brisbane bells operate under the Simpson 5 Tone System. The bell for sounding the hours weighs more than four tons and is almost seven feet in diameter. It tolls the note A-flat.

When city hall was opened in April 1930, the Melbourne *Argus* reported that 'the deep note of the clock as it boomed the hours' was one of the most memorable moments of the ceremony.

The former town hall, in Queen Street, still showed its own clock to Brisbane citizens despite the 'million-pound' city hall around the corner having opened for business. In 1933 a Kedron resident wrote a letter to the *Courier-Mail* complaining about the old timepiece. 'Either the clock should be put in order to show the correct time, be removed, or covered up so as not to be seen and so as not to mislead the public', wrote G.B. The letter writer was incensed that this thing 'which looks like a clock' had a face which 'lies to the public'. Indeed, the Queen Street hall had been the centre of debate since the late 19th century, its walls and ceilings cracking not long after construction. And now its clock was a liar.

From the viewing platform above the faces of the new city hall clock, you could see all the way to Mount Tibrogargan in the north, the Taylor Ranges to the west, Moreton Bay to the east, and the Stradbroke Islands to the south. It was the tallest building in Brisbane, holding the biggest clock in Australia. Residents set their home clocks to its A-flat chiming. In the mid-1930s its tolling was broadcast over the wireless, and Mrs Wilson, wife of Reverend Robert H. Wilson, a missionary on Mornington Island in the Gulf of Carpentaria, was just one who set her household clocks to this broadcast.

The clock tower of the city hall was a landmark for the residents of Brisbane for more than three decades, a spire, a maypole, a centre of gravity by which people could fix their location, their place, in this hilly, disorienting city, with its curling river and its steep, unpredictable hills. And it tolled in comforting harmony with Greenwich.

Nowadays from that same observation platform, at the base of the bells, the view in the direction of each of the four faces is broken and fragmented by mirrored skyscrapers. Some of them offer back a wobbly, distorted reflection of the clock tower itself.

To the east, you can glimpse, through a narrow canyon, the rough-hewn cliffs of the old Kangaroo Point quarry. To the south, walls of office blocks. To the west, the great hulk of the Catholic church at Red Hill and the blue-green Taylor Ranges. And to the north, cubed and dull office buildings and the tops of new riverside towers.

There are just two small slices of the Brisbane River visible from the tower – the ferry jetty at South Bank, and the little, grey, arched span of the Goodwill Bridge near the old dry dock. And completely obscured, just a few hundred metres away at North Quay, is the site where explorer John Oxley was supposed to have come ashore and founded the city of Brisbane.

On some days, it's impossible to hear the clock bells even when you're in the heart of the city. But on others, when the wind comes off the bay with the right strength and direction, and a myriad other factors in a modern metropolis fall into place, you can hear it drift into your wooden house. And on those rare occasions, you can be back when your grandmother quickened her step a little as she headed for the tram stop, the city hall clock singing her the time, or a neighbour turned over in bed, counting the hours until work the next day.

Or here, now, as a little boy, decades into this future, hears the chime through the Chinese elm tree out in the backyard and asks – 'What's that, Daddy?'

I am reading a story I wrote for a Sydney Saturday newspaper in 1996 and I'm no longer sure it's true anymore. I was living in that city and writing nostalgically about Brisbane. Throughout the long semi-autobiographical piece I refer to a Waterbury mantel clock that belonged to my grandmother Freda, and that was given to me when she was placed in a nursing home and her possessions dispersed. I wrote: 'For some unexplainable reason, the clock came to me.' Is this really what happened? It seems a phrase that has been lazily uncontemplated. I no longer know the voice in this story, the younger man who wrote it. He sounds inauthentic. 'I had never ever shown interest in it,' he says of the clock. 'As soon as it was taken from its home on the side cabinet,

it developed an erratic life of its own. It would remain dormant for weeks and suddenly, at 3am, it would emit twelve chimes, then stop again. Maybe six months would pass and it would decide at midday to ring out six chimes.' It reads as if the author is uncertain of his facts, or rounding them out to give them some sort of symmetry, or their own music. That he's building a myth around the timepiece. 'One month its hands would be set at 3.01. Then, secretively, sneakily, I would look at it again later and see that it had crept forward an hour, or 13 hours, or 37 hours, without a single chime. It had become an unhappy clock. A dislocated clock. It didn't like me and was transforming, in my eyes, into a piece of sentimental junk.' My grandmother, the little girl who came out on the S.S. Ormuz in 1925 and hated every day of her life in her new home of Brisbane, died a few months before I wrote this piece. It is shot through, I see now, with some sort of oblique grief. It is a splintered tribute, from a young man gone ten years from his home town, disconnected from it, and after a decade, the city, his city, has calcified in him, stopped in time, and this is the beginning of an expatriate's sentimental view of his place of birth. This is the point where he tips into nostalgia. This is when his relationship to his past changes. It is the first time he looks over his shoulder and sees a fairytale place, not a real city. And this, too, is when the accompanying long, low call of longing begins. I still have the Waterbury clock. It stopped its erratic behaviour at some point. It had to come home to Brisbane, and sit atop a bookshelf in a dining room not far from the chain of ponds, to stop completely. It ceased functioning at 5.29. I no longer pay it much attention. Recently, moving it during a small house renovation, I looked it unsentimentally in the face for the first time in years. It said 5.31.

'They were very, very unusual people.'

I am speaking on the telephone to June Cumbrae-Stewart, the 85-year-old daughter-in-law of F.W.S. Cumbrae-Stewart.

Just the day before, I'd decided to take a gamble and see if there were any descendants of F.W.S. living in Melbourne, where he died in 1938. How many Cumbrae-Stewarts could there be in the world? I started going through the directory list of just a few names. My first call was answered by a seemingly addled old gentleman who didn't have a clue what I was talking about. F.W.S? Never heard of him. Then my second call reached a young man who said I needed to talk to his Aunty June. Yes, F.W.S. and his wife Zina seemed to be in his family tree, as was the painter Janet Cumbrae-Stewart. Yes, they had some of her paintings hanging in the hallway. I left my number and the next day June phoned, from her home in Hobart.

'I'm sitting in the drawing room and it's exactly as it was, with their [F.W.S. and wife Zina's] wedding presents from 1906 . . . there's the revolving bookcase and the magnificent portrait of my mother-in-law in the tiara done by Janet, pictures by – Anyway, it's just a 1906 drawing room ... They were complete traditionalists, and apart from bringing the television set in here I've left it all as it was because it's, well, it's sort of them, you know?' she says. 'All my husband's father's books are here, you see. When I was on my honeymoon we were taken out to lunch by someone pretty high up in the Anglican church, and questions went backwards and forwards and so on, and everything my husband said was "my father said this" and "my father said that". This eminent figure said – "We've heard what your father thought about the soup and we've heard what your father thought about the meat, what did you think?"'

'Really, my husband just moulded himself on his father and his father's principles.'

Near the end of his life, F.W.S. returned with Zina to live near their only son, Francis Denys, in Melbourne. Several years later, Denys moved his household to Hobart. June, an accomplished academic, married Francis Denys well after his parents' deaths. But F.W.S.'s shadow is long, and Denys was a devoted son who could not bear to part with his parents' possessions. June still remembers the many stories of this man who had such a lasting impact on Brisbane.

F.W.S. was born at Riversleigh, Canterbury, in New Zealand, in 1865 before the Stewart family moved to Melbourne. The family home was called 'Montrose'. He was the eldest of ten children, the youngest being Janet Cumbrae-Stewart, who would later become a well-known painter in her day. F.W.S. studied in Oxford where he achieved second-class honours in history, and was called to the bar at London's Inner Temple in 1887. Returning to Melbourne, he practised at the Victorian Bar (1890–92) before moving to Brisbane where he practised from 1898 to 1903. From 1902 he edited the *Queensland State Report* (his son would later edit the Tasmanian law reports).

'He [F.W.S.] ended up in Brisbane because when he came back to Melbourne to practise after having been at Oxford, he was in the Owen Dixon Chambers in Melbourne, you see, and he really wasn't suitable for defending criminals or things like that, he was far too gentlemanly, far too polite, didn't know all the locals thugs and things ... then he got offered to be the first registrar of Queensland University.'

It was 1910 when F.W.S. became founding registrar and librarian of the University of Queensland. It was this event, it seems, that elevated the former Frank Stewart into the social and intellectual circles that he had craved. And Brisbane became his palette for a dizzying array of pursuits, from elite social events to membership of dozens of clubs and committees. He gave public lectures, wrote articles for the local newspapers and magazines, organised graduation ceremonies for the university. He was also building his credentials as a local historian.

Just two years after being appointed registrar, Frank Stewart curiously changed his surname. Was it not big enough for the rockpool that was Brisbane? Was it not sufficiently regal for a university registrar and librarian? According to Brisbane historian Jean Stewart, F.W.S. had a passion for his own genealogy.

As she writes in her book *Scribblers*, an account of a women's writing group in Brisbane that included Zina Cumbrae-Stewart: 'Foremost among his hobbies was genealogical research and he became chief of the Kincardine branch of the Stewarts of Bute in 1908. The Cumbrae in his name, which he added to the Stewart with a hyphen although some other members of his family did not, comes from two islands on the west coast of Scotland … There is doubtful evidence of the family's ancestry in that area but F.W.S. Cumbrae-Stewart felt that his research made a possible connection. A letter from the Heralds College, London dated 13 May 1912, indicated that he applied to assume an additional surname.'

The affectation – if it was one – was not missed by his students at the University of Queensland, then housed in the CBD. As Jean Stewart continues, the following verse appeared in the Degree Day of 1928 'Programme and Song Book' to the tune of 'Mush, Mush, Mush, too-a-li-addy':

Cumbrae, K.C.

Stewart. That name was untarnished
When first he was called to the Bar;
But his name with a 'Cumbrae' was garnished
When he came as our first Registrar.

June Cumbrae-Stewart confirms F.W.S.'s higher

aspirations for himself and his family. 'The whole thing is that the old man, F.W.S, when he has a son, becomes intensely interested in proving he was from Robert the Bruce, you see,' she says. But 'if the link is there it would be in actual fact illegitimate. The person he's supposed to be descended from, there wasn't any sign of a marriage, you see.' He supposedly once remarked that if not for a little 'misfortune' his line of Stewarts would have occupied the English throne.

According to the *Australian Dictionary of Biography*, Cumbrae-Stewart was 'severe, with an erect military bearing and a fiercely waxed moustache … he was always formal and pontifical in public. Although he mellowed with age, he attracted respect rather than affection.'

Historian Helen Gregory wrote of Cumbrae-Stewart as the university registrar being 'rigid and authoritarian', and that his 'commanding physical presence was daunting'.

With his passion for history, F.W.S. also became one of the founding fathers of the Queensland Historical Society in 1913. He and University of Queensland lecturer A.C.V. Melbourne formed a provisional committee earlier that year and the society was formally launched in August. Former premier Sir Arthur Morgan was elected president, and F.W.S. vice-president. In April the following year, at the society's first general meeting, F.W.S. delivered the inaugural lecture, 'The Memorials in St John's Cathedral'. He edited the early issues of the society's journals, and wrote many papers. In early 1917, after the death of Morgan, F.W.S. was elected president, and held the post until 1930.

The almost Scottish royal, however, may not have been the ideal choice for a provincial historical society. In a paper titled 'The Politics of Preserving the Past: The Early Years of the Historical Society of Queensland' by Peter Biskup, F.W.S.'s regal demeanour is seen to have put more than a few noses out of joint.

'While he may have been an asset to a new and raw university where his "punctilious ceremoniousness" made up for the lack of tradition, he was the wrong person to preside over the meetings of elderly descendants of Queensland pioneers, most of whom found his authoritarianism and "pompous mannerisms and excessive dignity" irritating. He was not one of them and did not command their respect. The resignation of no less than twelve members during the first years of his presidency may have been no mere coincidence.'

Only one meeting of the society was held in 1924. It was to celebrate the hundredth anniversary of the discovery of the site of Brisbane. The president addressed the society, 'basing his remarks upon Mr Oxley's field books and identifying the spots where he landed, especially the place at North Quay...'

So here we are, getting closer to F.W.S.'s interest in the Brisbane River and his unwavering belief that Oxley landed at North Quay and not further north along the reach of the river at Milton. I needed to examine his writings.

I am playing with my son and our bitsa dog Charley in the unleashed canine park opposite Suncorp Stadium in Milton. It is the first day of sunshine after a week of rain, and dogs and owners before us have muddied up the park. When the government redeveloped the grounds in the late 1990s, demolishing the old Lang Park football stadium, it deployed the University of Queensland Archaeological Services Unit to examine the subsurface deposits. The area was once the North Brisbane Burial Grounds, and accepted Brisbane's dead from 1843 to 1875. When the land was rezoned for sport and recreation in 1910, relatives of the deceased were

informed and about 150 remains were exhumed. From late 2000 to mid-2001 the archaeological team exhumed almost 400 burials, including three intact coffins. According to team experts, in many of the children's graves the coffin wood and bone had become 'little more than dark stains in the subsoil'. On our day of play, a foul odour hovered about the muddy park. 'Sewage,' I say out loud to myself. 'No, Dad,' my boy says, 'that smells like skeletons.'

On another day the boy went to see his friend Bill who lived in a green wooden house on the edge of a park not far from the city. Bill was a boy who could build things. He was also handy on the guitar, good with animals (he wanted to be a veterinarian) and was big enough and tall enough to be a permanent fixture in the school's First XV for his age group.

For months Bill had been building a two-man kayak of his own design, and he laboured relentlessly underneath his house, sanding and lacquering. On this day when the boy arrived Bill had finished the kayak. The polished wood glowed like pale honey.

'We should go for a paddle next weekend,' Bill said.

And the following Sunday Bill and the boy were driven down to the Brisbane River and they set off.

Bill's parents were urban hippies, precursors to today's Greenies, if having a goat tethered in the backyard for milk and growing your own vegetables made you a hippie. It was the early 1970s. Our boy's parents, though, carried the residue of the '50s. There were no vegetables in their own garden, above the ancient boulders. His vegetables came from the back of an old Bedford truck driven by a man in a large, battered cane hat. He was called Mr Green. Mr Green went from street to street in his truck with the scales and battered tin scale dish swinging out the back. The boy always thought Mr Green was the farmer who grew all those crates full of produce. Then Mr Green vanished when they built a Woolworths down near Walton Bridge. And the records in the boy's house were Sinatra and 'The King and I', not Dylan and Young and Yes. Once, the boy dressed up as a 'hippie' for the annual school concert, and his mother had very carefully drawn a peace symbol on the front of his white T-shirt, and he wore a large curly wig and beads around his neck, and it felt like what it was – dress-ups – because 'hippies' were never seen in real life where he lived in the colonial house.

Bill was a foot taller than the boy and had caught from his parents a free-wheeling spirit with his passion for sailing and other aquatic sports and the guitar and his deftness at milking a goat.

But a journey up the Brisbane River with Bill in that kayak was an exciting prospect to the boy, so that Sunday they pushed off somewhere close to the city for a leisurely two-hour paddle around the winding river to landfall near the University of Queensland at St Lucia.

Somewhere along the way, though, they lost their bearings. One moment they were paddling west, then east, and at another turn south-east, then south-west, then north. After two hours they couldn't find St Lucia, so Bill, the captain of the vessel, deemed they continue on until they reached a familiar landmark.

The boy admired the riverside houses, their long yards and wooden jetties. He wondered what it would be like to live on the river, especially at night; what might you hear through your bedroom window beside a river? Lots of waterfowl and frogs and the splash of a fish, he thought, instead of the blinking sacred lights of the television towers. They paddled for another hour, and then there were fewer houses, and the foliage on the bends and turns looked wild and bedraggled. The river, after several hours, had narrowed, and there were shadows across its broken surface. The boy's arms were so sore he could barely raise the paddle. The sun was falling behind the hills, and the sky was flaming orange, and the darkness in the mangroves on either side of them looked dangerous.

It was frightening, then, the dark river and the banks of impenetrable lantana, the tight, prickly wall of it beyond the mangroves. The boy didn't say anything to Bill, paddling away in front of him. He didn't want Bill to know he was scared. This was not the boy's city anymore, but a storybook jungle that yielded no shoreline. In fact, the banks of the river seemed intent on keeping the boy and Bill away and on the water. He had never seen Brisbane from this vantage point. It was inhospitable. It was cruel.

At dusk they eased around yet another bend and in the distance saw a bridge and cleared land at the water's edge. They came ashore, hungry, thirsty and exhausted. They did not know where they were. They had to find someone to ask. They were told they were in the suburb of Goodna, halfway to Ipswich. They telephoned their parents from a phone box using coins wrapped in the corners of checked handkerchiefs, and were retrieved an hour later.

The boy felt uncomfortable waiting for his parents in Goodna as evening fell. He was still full of the cold shock of being lost, and waiting there in the dull light of the phone box, part of him had yet to be found, had yet to reach safety. He was disturbed, too, because he knew all about Goodna.

Everyone in Brisbane did. Goodna, for decades, housed the city's mental institution. Every city has its madhouse, and Goodna was Brisbane's. When you mentioned the word 'Goodna', people knew precisely what you were talking about. Goodna was a creepy word. It was a word that existed in isolation, and had all sorts of hollow space around it, and shadows behind it. Goodna meant unhappiness and tears and sadness and unpredictable people. His own grandmother had been a patient there for several months from November 1940. Though the boy wouldn't know this for decades, she was diagnosed with post-natal depression after the birth of the boy's mother, and suffered recurrent bouts of illness from that moment for the rest of her life.

Even on the day of the kayak up the river, waiting in the security of the phone-box light, he had an eerie feeling he had been here before, to

Goodna, and that he had sat with people dressed in soft white gowns on a lawn, and been very quiet as he was told to be quiet, and tried not to stare at anything. He wasn't sure if he'd ever been there before, as a little boy.

At the phone box he was very quiet and didn't stare at anything, and he stayed like that all the way home to the little colonial perched above the ancient boulders.

My grandmother Freda's illness, like many things in our family, was one of those matters that were never really discussed, but you always knew it was there, like an old car under canvas in the shed out the back.

On many occasions in my 20s I had visited her, with my mother, in various hospital wards across Brisbane, then in a succession of nursing homes, and was sitting by her bedside, holding her right hand, when she died in 1996. Moments after death all the worry and fear and sadness vanished from her face, and she was beautiful.

Recently I made tentative steps to recover the story of her time in Goodna's mental hospital. I was told that despite the fact she was no longer alive, patient records remained confidential. Still, someone at the records department emailed me a photograph of my grandmother taken on her admission in 1940. It arrived in my computer as one of those little red-flecked electronic attachments.

I double-clicked and there she was, in her early 20s and dressed in an institution smock, her thick wavy hair dishevelled, her face bearing a partial smile through what seemed to me an enormous countenance of pain. I recognised her and I didn't. I had never seen the youthful figure and the chestnut hair, but I had seen the pain behind the pale, fragile English skin of her face.

I have stared and stared at this picture ever since. I think of her husband George at their home in Beck Street, Rosalie, and her newborn baby — my mother — being looked after by an aunt. I can see George downstairs at night at his workbench in the yellow glow of a light bulb, and her brother Tom, living across the street from them, sitting down to his dinner at his small rectangular kitchen table, and Mrs Guy, on the corner, preparing meat and vegetables for her children and thinking of Freda, and I can see Rodney, the mentally handicapped boy, making his tenth, his twentieth, lap of the block, oblivious to the world, and Mrs Carten, a few doors down, standing at her own Kooka in a floral nylon dress and thinking of Freda, and the street quiet, except for the distant chimes of the city hall clock passing through the mauve jacarandas and across the chain of ponds and into the wooden Queenslanders, reminding those in Beck Street, on this night, not of the time of day, but of life's fragility and its incremental march forward.

I realise suddenly that I might be the first person in my family to see this almost 70-year-old photograph. Perhaps the only person to have seen it outside the Goodna institution.

It had been sitting in a filing cabinet, pinned to a patient's index card with my grandmother's name on it, for all that time. It was inside the cabinet, unseen, when Bill and I scrambled ashore at Goodna that day in his honey-coloured kayak. It was there, pressed in the dark, as I waited in the light of the phone box. It was there when my two children were born and brought home, to the house just a five-minute walk to Beck Street.

Will I ever show it to them? And what will I say? This was your great-grandmother, who when she was a young girl arrived in Brisbane by boat from the other side of the world, like our early explorers and settlers, and never got to go home again. This was your great-grandmother, when she became ill. This was Freda, who lived most of her life in a subtropical city in Australia, who thought always of the snow when she was little, and passed away in a drab, chilly air-conditioned hospital room not far from the Pacific Ocean, before you were born.

Oxley was charged by Governor Brisbane to survey Moreton Bay and other sites with a view to establishing convict settlements, and on October 23, 1823, set off from Sydney in the H.M.Cutter *Mermaid*. On Saturday, November 29, the *Mermaid* nosed into Moreton Bay and dropped anchor.

Incredibly, on that same day Oxley and his crew rescued a white castaway, Thomas Pamphlet, who, along with John Finnegan and Richard Parsons (all ticket-of-leave convicts), had been shipwrecked on Moreton Island several months earlier. They were sailing from Sydney to the Illawarra to collect timber when a gale blew them off course and hundreds of miles north. They had lived with the local blacks. As Pamphlet narrated of the trio's hosts, 'Their behaviour to me and my companions had been so invariably kind and generous that, notwithstanding the delight I felt at the idea of once more returning to my home, I did not leave them without sincere regret.'

Finnegan was rescued the following day (Parsons not until the following year, as the party had earlier split up) and told Oxley of a large river in the area. The castaways had stumbled across it in June, and explored it as far as present-day Tennyson. Oxley and Lieutenant Stirling (Oxley's first assistant, and author of the first map of the Brisbane River) set off the next day to find the river, with Finnegan as their guide. Finnegan couldn't relocate it – but the experienced Oxley did, and they headed up river as far as today's Goodna, before returning to the bay and back to Sydney.

Oxley was back the following year with Commandant Miller and about thirty convicts aboard the brig *Amity*, and was also accompanied by botanist Allan Cunningham and surveyor Robert Hoddle. On September 17, Oxley and Cunningham set out to explore the river more extensively. Within days Oxley found his 'chain of ponds'.

That November Oxley returned again, accompanying Governor Brisbane on an inspection to found the city that would at first be named 'Edenglassie'. In his 1823 report, Oxley had recommended Breakfast Creek as the settlement site, but his 1824 expedition in a time of drought declared the area devoid of decent water. Nevertheless, the mouth of Breakfast Creek was deemed the site following Oxley and the Governor's visit, and it wasn't until the following year that the colony was relocated further around the bends of the river to William Street and the reach where the Oxley obelisk now stands.

As Governor Brisbane left what would become his namesake city, he sensed a lost opportunity with the local indigenous people. The *Sydney Gazette* reported on December 9, 1824, 'His Excellency regretted that the Expedition had not earlier fallen in with these aborigines, that some degree of confidence might have been commenced upon, if not established, between them and the Europeans. They are evidently of a superior order to those in the Southern part of this continent.'

In the vicinity at the time, as head of the North Pine tribe – part of the Gubbi Gubbi people – would have been Dalipie or Dalaipi. He was in his early 50s when Oxley first interrogated the landscape. A generation afterwards he was described by Tom Petrie in his *Reminiscences of Early Queensland* as 'not an extra tall blackfellow, but was good and very reverent looking, and carried himself with an air as though he were someone of importance, as, indeed he was, for his word was law among the tribe, and he was looked up to by everyone… he was very gentle and courteous, and never seemed to join in with a rough joke.' Petrie noted 'he was the only blackfellow I knew who neither smoked nor drank'.

Petrie's memoirs detail some wonderful discussions he shared with Dalipie/Dalaipi about the impact of white settlement on the indigenous population.

Long after Oxley's visits, in late 1858 and early 1859, on the eve of the settlement's secession from the state of New South Wales, a series of extraordinary letters was published in the *Moreton Bay Courier*, attributed to Dalipie and Dalinkua – 'Delegates for all blackfellows. Camp. Breakfast Creek.'

The five letters to the editor amount to a clear, logical, and emotionally devastating treatise on the phrase *terra nullius*, as we know it, and a convincing argument for native title, before this, too, entered the lexicon. In a few deft strokes the letters exposed the social and spiritual hammer blow that European settlement had delivered to the local indigenous people. It is shocking to read them today. Their appeal for humanity is brilliantly delivered, paced to perfection, and builds across the weeks between publication to a final condemnation of biblical wrath.

The first letter – published on Wednesday, November 17, 1858 – begins on a note of self-analysis. 'Far back in the unexplored annals of antiquity – sacred now owing to distance – the curse of indolence settled on our ancestors; and we inherited from them all that rust which ages have gathered and thickened on our minds, so that we cannot open them. The darkness of centuries has stunted, dwarfed, and killed our intellects. All of man that was in us was so fettered that we became more and more stupid and indocile [sic], as one generation succeeded another, until we reached the lowest platform of society, where we have lain stagnant in sluggish torpor until now.'

It is a pitiable scenario. It is sorrowful. It is a sketch of the fall of man. It goes on, 'All of humanity, all of intellectuality, are long since dead and gone from us for want of exercise; animal gratification was all we or our people desired. No example of industry did we get from our fathers, except when hunger compelled us to hunt, or fierce and revengeful feeling urged us to fight.'

What would the readers of the *Moreton Bay Courier* have made of this frank exposition? Look at us, it says, we are as you see us and this is the explanation. You can imagine white folk in the coffee houses or yarning at the horse bazaar in Queen Street or drinking at a nearby inn thinking or saying – of course we were right, they are indolent savages, useless, worthless. Look, they admit it themselves.

Then the letter changes tone. 'Sir, this Anglo-

Saxon brought with him a "book of books," containing the laws and commands of the high and the holy One, who was father of all, black and white; and we were all brothers, all to love one another. It said the naked were to be clothed and the hungry were to be fed. We were overjoyed at this. It was also to enlighten by its light every man and woman. How suitable for our darkness ... and to crown the whole, we were told that love was the fulfilling of the whole of this law. That white fellow love us; and we were told that the Great Father was everywhere present to see that his children observed all things whatsoever he had commanded them.'

You can see, a century and a half later, what Dalipie and Dalinkua are doing here – they have moved inside the white settler's heads, first with the opening self-criticism and next into the heart of their faith, their belief system. The white man brought the 'book of books'. The white man believes in the Great Father and his laws and commands. If that is the white man's belief, then God is watching over all that he does.

'But, Sir', they continue, 'these Anglo-Saxons have not behaved towards us as if they believed that His eye was on them who has given them more knowledge than any other nation, also a loftier civilisation. All the above laws have they trampled on, and we are sorry to have to impeach them before high heaven of crimes and misdemeanours.'

In this first letter they conclude that the offenders will suffer 'many and terrible counts in that indictment which shall be brought to the bar of the Judge of the Universe'.

'We have spoken!' the letter ends bravely. 'If you hear us, we will speak next week more to our white brothers, and read their indictment.'

It is not just thrilling newspaper copy – which white brother wouldn't want to tune in next week to hear the indictments against him, and from the local blacks, of all people? – but a superbly realised argument. The delegates' audience, in the end, have been reduced to something they understand, to children of God. Who is civilised or uncivilised now?

On Wednesday, November 24, the second letter – containing the indictments brought before the 'bar of Universal Justice' – begins with a volley of explosive truths. 'These, our white brothers, have taken our hunting and fishing grounds from us, that spot of earth from which we and our fathers obtained food, which was all we required; and they have not made any provision to preserve us from starvation. They, the strongest nation on earth, have taken from the weakest nation the domain of their ancestors, and they have driven away defence-less fellow creatures to banishments, hardship and death.'

The authors then discuss the legality of owner-ship of land, or absence of it. 'Now how did our pale-faced brother obtain our land? Not by con-quest for no one opposed him! Not by cession, for no parties that we know off [sic] could cede it to him; but being possessed of power and knowledge, and we being weak and ignorant, he merely ran it over with a theodolite, a chain, a hatchet and some pegs or some marks on trees — their titles patent from the Queen, it thus became his property and we may starve, unless we skulk about and spear cattle.'

The delegates counter arguments that they have forfeited their land because they do not make 'use of it'. They speak of indigenous people not wanting to 'subdue' the land, but using only as much as they need. They wonder if white settle-ment has made them feel they are 'here by some mistake'. They say that if, as in India for example, their country had been 'defended by gods', then the government would have 'endowed them, and their priests and pagadoes'. But 'we have no national gods', they conclude.

The third letter (Saturday, December 11, 1858) explicates the ravages of alcohol and disease wrought on the indigenous community. 'Look at our bodies, made like your own, all but the skin ... see how many of us are disgusting spectacles, rotting with putrefaction while still living ... see also our wretched offspring, masses of putrid sores while yet at their mother's breast ... '

A fourth letter, printed on Saturday, January 8, 1859, continues outlining political injustice. 'If we had a Pagoda at the Bunya Bunya scrub, having a wooden Bunyip to worship as the hero of plenty, surrounded by devotees and frequented by pilgrims, we should have a grant of land for the benefit of the staff required to keep the idol shrine and funds from the government for the idol festivals.'

It finishes: 'Christians, you are here in this land by the inscrutable Providence of God! Have you brought your religion with you?'

The fifth and final missive, published on Wednesday, January 26, 1859 – a calendar date we celebrate today for different reasons – ends in both hope and despair. 'Although the churches expect that every professed disciple will do his duty attaching to his profession, and duties also which are inalienably attached to property, you who have acquired property in Australia, to what extent have you discharged those duties which are contingent with your rights?'

The letters – written and published just three decades after the 'discovery' of Brisbane – are an early snapshot of indigenous conditions. Moreso, they are a plea in the wilderness for justice and human rights, and they echo through the centuries to contemporary Australia. They are first-class reporting and intellectual commentary. They transcend the age of their creation.

In the second of the three letters, Dalipie's name is incorrectly spelt *Dalipia*. Each letter is headlined 'ABORIGINES'. But they didn't seem to illicit any written responses from the community at large. Perhaps the indictments were too close to the bone for the 6000 or so white settlers in Brisbane. Besides, the populace had preparations for secession at hand, and a new governor, Sir George Bowen, to welcome at the end of the year with fireworks and music and river regattas.

In early February, 1859, the letters did provoke a comment from a *Courier* columnist – 'A Sydney Man' – in his 'News and Notes' report. He was writing about a proposal to give Aborigines the vote, saying it may be of interest 'to those aboriginal curiosities of yours, Dalinkua and Dalipie, who may thus see a chance of becoming "delegates" to our talking-shop in Macquarie street', where they 'might continue to talk nonsense without being much put out of countenance'.

Were the letters literally written by the two men, or transcribed and shaped by well-meaning local missionaries or town journalists hoping to expose the appalling conditions suffered by the region's indigenous population?

I contact Alex Bond, a descendant of Dalipie's people, who lives on Queensland's Sunshine Coast.

'They are important documents, regardless of people saying he [Dalipie] couldn't possibly have written them himself,' says Alex. 'The feelings and emotions and instances definitely come from an Aboriginal person.

'Dalipie would have been well-educated by 1858. His knowledge of the big world would have been more. You can't say who penned the letters. I don't think he would have penned them himself. I think some narration and a discussion with a third party went on. That is acceptable to me but perhaps not other people in terms of what they believe, you know?

'I'd really like to believe they wrote them, but it's a strong belief of mine that they sat down and there would have been other people there, some Englishman columnist in amongst that group of people. Having said that, there were a lot of educated Aboriginal people back then. People don't realise that.'

In 1995 – 136 years after the letters were published – a research project into the retention of Aboriginal and Torres Strait Islander males in tertiary study was conducted in Brisbane, titled 'The Dalipie & Dalinkua Project'.

The preface of the final report said, 'Because of these two men's stance on social justice and fair play for all Australians, their commitment to improving the lives of Aboriginal people and for the excellent role models they serve, and for their character marked by truth and justice, we are proud to have been granted the permission to use their names to call our project.'

Apart from this acknowledgment, Dalipie and Dalinkua have been forgotten.

When the Brisbane City Council ran a public internet contest in 2009, asking residents what name they would like to give the new Hale Street bridge, linking Milton on the northside of the

Brisbane River just a stone's throw from the Oxley obelisk, with South Brisbane, hundreds of titles were suggested. They ranged from the John Howard Bridge (after the former prime minister), the Joh Bjelke-Petersen Bridge (after the former premier), the Wally Lewis Bridge (after the former rugby league player), the Wayne Bennett Bridge (after the former Brisbane Broncos rugby league coach), the Gunsynd Bridge (after the racehorse), the Fourex Bridge (after the beer), the Bundy Bridge (after the rum), the Stefan Bridge (after the local Brisbane celebrity hairdresser) and the Hope You're Home at a Decent Time Now Bridge (with a wink to Brisbane's peak-hour traffic).

One person nominated the 'Daliapi Bridge': 'During the 1840s and 1850s, he was an important bridge builder between the white and black communities, and a fiery commentator on environmental degradation and mistreatment of indigenous folk'.

On September 29, 2009, it was announced that the bridge would be called the Go Between Bridge, after a local pop music band.

F.W.S. Cumbrae-Stewart had written papers on early Brisbane history and the river specifically. In 1923 he had published, in the *Brisbane Courier*, a short biography of Lieutenant Henry Miller, who moved the settlement up from Redcliffe to the site at North Quay. F.W.S. seemed fascinated with Miller.

However the historical society's Brisbane River meeting of 1924, was to be its last for five years. In late 1925, F.W.S. applied for and won the Garrick Professor of Law chair at the university. At about the same time he became co-trustee of the Oxley Centenary Fund. It seems his interest in the society began to wane from this point. Though he was happy to be lumbered with responsibility for the mooted granite monument and John Oxley library.

According to Peter Biskup, writing on F.W.S. in the *Journal of the Royal Historical Society of Queensland* (November, 1988), 'despite being an "almost compulsive scribbler", he published no substantial work either before or after' taking up the chair of professor of law. Indeed, as June Cumbrae-Stewart says, 'He was a prolific writer. He wrote a great deal about Queensland law, but he didn't write any books or anything. He wrote a lot of pamphlets.'

I decide to head out to the Fryer Library to

look through their holdings of F.W.S. Cumbrae-Stewart's papers. Could there be a solid clue there as to his insistence the John Oxley memorial be placed at North Quay? How had he made this mistake?

This morning I am the only person in the library, which is not too far from the Cumbrae-Stewart Building (opened in 1983 by then governor Sir Walter Campbell) on the university campus. That building was, for a time, famous for its leaky roof and possum inhabitants.

One of the first documents I retrieve from the F.W.S. files is his 'History of Brisbane River'. It is a handwritten series of notes and lengthy passages about Oxley's second journey up the river in 1924 that seem to have been taken from the Field Books. There is another fragment: 'The *Amity* has on board Lt. Miller ... and the 40th Regt and the party went up to form the view ... ' And there it ends.

His 'History of Queensland' is another cluster of notes written on the back of university course papers and even invitations to events he organised, such as the Citizens Farewell to Archbishop Donaldson. 'RSVP to ... Mr Cumbrae-Stewart.' There are thoughts and ideas scribbled on the back of a

Brisbane Diocesan Synod nomination form. On one of his papers he has drawn an elaborate cannon.

If this is a snapshot of F.W.S.'s mind more than 80 years ago, it's a mind that is rushed, perhaps fevered, scribbling dot points and ideas on any paper at hand, largely without logic or order. The thick half-A4 wads of handwritten papers are the work of a man not writing in the first instance for publication but for verbal delivery. Here, then, are his historical society lectures and notes for talks and articles. He was, in large part, a performer, and these were his scripts. There is no evidence of original historical research. No records of interviews with living pioneers or references to other historical sources. They appear to be summaries of things written by others.

In a handwritten passage under the words 'Brisbane' and 'Choice of Site', he writes, 'It is clear from Oxley's map and his description of the spot that the site... is at the junction of the river and Breakfast Creek. When the –' And the thought runs out again. He has even written a date, '1824 Aug', then struck out 'Aug' and replaced it with 'Sept'.

There is nothing in the papers to corroborate F.W.S.'s incorrect siting of the John Oxley obelisk.

Then the Queensland Newspapers archivist

shows me a copy of an article written by 'Dr Cumbrae Stewart' in the special Christmas edition of the *Queenslander* magazine, published on December 1, 1923. His piece, headlined 'Did Oxley Land at Newstead? Evidence in Oxley's Diary', accompanies several extracts from Oxley's Field Books for early December, 1823. F.W.S. debates the explorer's initial investigations of the river and concludes Oxley's first suggested long-term settlement site for the city was at Breakfast Creek, which few historians have ever disputed, before F.W.S. or since.

However, he later writes, 'There does not appear to be any evidence that he landed anywhere else near the present site of the city until his return from his second journey up the river in September, 1824, when it would appear that he landed somewhere near the upper end of North Quay to look for water which, he says, "we found in abundance and of excellent quality, being at this season a chain of ponds watering a fine valley… by no means an ineligible station for a first settlement up the river".'

Here, F.W.S. publishes for the first time his belief that Miller's chosen site for settlement at North Quay and the chain of ponds in Oxley's Field Books are linked. His choice of phrase – 'it would appear' – shows the same lack of confidence as the wording on the plaque. It's possible that this article may have given F.W.S. the public intellectual kudos to become so intrinsically involved in the planning of the obelisk. Just over two months later the Queensland governor, Sir Matthew Nathan, made his extraordinary plea to the Brisbane Centenary Celebrations Committee for some form of monument to be erected in memory of Oxley's discovery of the city. (F.W.S. was well acquainted with Nathan. There are several surviving photographs of them together, including a group portrait of the Brisbane Dickens Fellowship where Sir Matthew is seated centre front, and F.W.S. is just two seats to his right. As well, Zina Cumbrae-Stewart's nephew, Henry Hammond, was Aide-de-Camp to Nathan.)

Less than a week after I read the *Queenslander* article, F.W.S.'s creation – the now-named Royal Historical Society of Queensland (I can't help but think he would have approved of and enjoyed the regal imprimatur) – email me a small document written by Cumbrae-Stewart himself and published in the society's journal of October 23, 1925. It is, of sorts, a brief summary of the society's activities over the preceding few years, a loose annual report that tidies up business.

It reads, in hindsight, as something of a farewell from Cumbrae-Stewart to the society, as he moves on to the law chair at the university. It details his fervour for celebrating Oxley's achievements and the river itself. It gives a brief report on a social function in late 1923 to commemorate Oxley's discovery of the Brisbane River.

And it takes us into the rooms of the Brisbane Women's Club in the old *Courier* building at the corners of Queen and Edward streets, in September 1924, when the historical society celebrated the centenary of Oxley's discovery of the city.

It was here that Cumbrae-Stewart cemented his error and gave our city book a fragment of index that couldn't be trusted.

'He was absolutely tremendous on detail,' June says of her father-in-law.

But he wasn't on that warm spring Saturday in the heart of the city, a five-minute walk to the future site of the five-ton obelisk on the bank of the Brisbane River.

When novelist Gilbert Parker arrived in Brisbane by train from Sydney in 1889, he was instantly struck by the 'crisp tender air' and the 'mellow sun-warmth' which he said filled him with wonderment.

Parker was taking notes for a book he was preparing – *Round the Compass of Australia* – and from the outset he was unimpressed with Brisbane's architecture.

'No', he wrote, 'Brisbane is not the least poetical. Brisbane is in appearance scraggy, low-built, and premature. It is far from picturesque as a whole, and first impressions are not changed by closer inspection. There is a sense of disappointment, which grows deeper as the sojourn in the capital is continued. One gets the impression now of a town that is but half-dressed ... '

Parker adopts the age-old method of a reporter arriving in a strange town – he gets his background material from the cab driver. In Parker's case, he jotted down the immortal thoughts of his 'carman': 'It's Parlimint that's ruining us, sir; if we could give Sir Sam'l [Sir Samuel Griffith] ten years' hard, things would get evener again. You see, he's always got some fad, and cracks things up, and we puts our bloomin' quids into it; and there you are!'

Parker's greatest complaint was the city's lack of trees. Trees, thought Parker, would make a half-dressed city look at least decently clothed. 'Twenty-five thousand trees would make Brisbane beautiful. They would glorify its nakedness; they would give it altitude; they would bring something of moisture, comfort and health.'

He was not happy either with the overall conceptual design of the city, and this has been something debated in bedrooms and ballrooms since Lieutenant Miller, in his wisdom, decided to strategically place the settlement on the high side of the horseshoe that is Gardens Point.

It is as if the city site has, since its inception, constantly resisted the myriad plans and dreams that have been laid over it for almost 200 years. Did the confusion regarding Oxley's 'chain of ponds' at the very start, the indecision, forever implant the place with a sort of irritated, restless gene, and does it riffle through the earth beneath the CBD to this day?

The inevitability of the convict settlement putting down some form of roots by the nature of its very existence — fetid little rockpool that it was, huddled on the horseshoe — and the reluctance to change location *again*, were most likely the origins of the city's geographical birth, as opposed to a decision that looked clearly into the future. Limestone Hills (later known as Ipswich) was also vying for the title of principal settlement. And Cleveland Point was eyed as an alternative port to Brisbane.

Miller was dismissed in August 1825, just months after relocating the settlement, and was replaced by Captain Peter Bishop. According to W. Ross Johnston's *Brisbane: the First Thirty Years*, Bishop 'was anxious to settle in and give an air of permanency to the place; so he started building.' But by March the following year Bishop too was replaced, by Captain Patrick Logan. 'After familiarising himself with the bay he concluded that the penal establishment had been badly placed', wrote Johnston. 'It was too far up the river, and in particular there was the difficulty of crossing the bar at its mouth.'

In 1827 Logan proposed moving the settlement again, to Dunwich on Stradbroke Island. When NSW Governor Ralph Darling visited Moreton Bay that year, he too queried the settlement site. 'The tediousness and difficulty of the access render it extremely inconvenient', Darling wrote.

Despite Logan's agitation with the site, he was responsible for the erection of the convict windmill on Wickham Terrace and the Commissariat Store in William Street, the only two convict-era structures that stand today in the modern city. Ultimately, the site controversy waned as talk gathered momentum through the 1830s that the convict outpost would soon end and be thrown open to free settlement.

Still, a decade or so of civilisation on Miller's patch of folly had created a small, serviceable grid of human perambulation. 'By this stage some major thoroughfares had emerged in the township through regular usage – down to the government garden, from the barn to the river, from the Commissariat store to the burial grounds, from the Commandant's residence to the hospital, lumber yard, prisoners' barrack and beyond', wrote Johnston.

This then, was the first Brisbane city template, trampled out by people seeking food or tending to it, burying their dead, retrieving goods from the riverbank, hurrying about their daily business. As the convict experiment wound down, so did the buildings associated with it. By the late 1830s many of them were in disrepair. Serendipitously, the colony's plea to Sydney for a competent builder to remedy the problem in 1837 was met with the appointment of Scottish immigrant Andrew Petrie as clerk of works to Moreton Bay. The industrious Petrie, a builder and architect, drew up his own set of plans for Brisbane Town, that in turn were adopted by Major George Barney of the Royal Engineers in Sydney, who also drafted a town plan.

Major Sydney Cotton, the settlement's sixth commandant, who took charge in 1839, seemed the right man for the job of opening the colony to free settlers. He and Petrie were soon working in concert for a planned future for Brisbane. Meanwhile, young Tom Petrie was off playing at the Aboriginal camp, where the RNA Showgrounds are now.

In 1839, also, Sydney sent up three surveyors – Robert Dixon, James Warner and Granville Stapylton – to accurately survey Brisbane Town and its surrounds with a theodolite. Governor Sir George Gipps was pleased that scientific surveying was at last being applied to Brisbane, 'and not made, as I regret to say all former Surveys have been, by the compass instead of the Theodolite'. By early 1840, Dixon had finally committed to paper the first real survey of the town: as Johnston wrote, 'A grid pattern of square blocks (ten chains in length) with streets 66 feet wide. These streets were based upon the prisoners' barrack as the main alignment and cut across the existing tracks that had arisen over the years.' So there we have it. The fulcrum of the future city was its criminal past.

And the mind from which the city layout sprang? What of Dixon, born in the market town of Darlington, county Durham, north of Leeds in the United Kingdom? The rivers Tees and Skerne pass through the town. Did he put a little of Darlington into Brisbane? After his grid was drawn he was promoted to surveyor-general of Moreton Bay, but then had a falling out with the town's last commandant, Lieutenant Owen Gordon. Dixon was suspended in 1841 after an altercation over the arrest of his convict servant. In the same year he published his own map of Moreton Bay, infuriating Governor Gipps. Then, when the settlement was finally opened up in 1842, he applied for leases on several government buildings, and was rejected. He left the colony and briefly settled in Toongabbie, west of Parramatta, where he continued his surveying work with little success. A petty skirmish in Brisbane – the town he laid out – dramatically changed the course of his life. He was dead at 58.

One of his many legacies, though, would be the Brisbane Town template, though it was modified shortly after by another surveyor, Henry Wade, the squares being replaced by a rectangular grid and the streets widened. The pesky Gipps visited the town in 1842 and ordered the streets be trimmed back. Brisbane, thought Gipps, was provincial and didn't need grand avenues. It had a future only as 'a paltry village'. He reasoned that by bringing the buildings on either side of a thoroughfare closer together in this subtropical place, it would block out the sun and induce drafts. In the grid, the streets cross-hatch, British queens running in one direction, kings in the other. If you look at an aerial view of the CBD, the streets neatly strafe across the inside of the horseshoe.

As Johnston noted, and as Gilbert Parker would whine about, little consideration was given to reserve areas. The point of land on which the city sat was so restricted 'it seems that the planners con-templated that as much area as possible, apart from the government garden already set aside, should be used for various building purposes… serious criti-cism was made later of the failure to reserve river frontage for public purposes'.

So the city was set. It had little room for trees and parkland. Why broad avenues, for a place that had no substantial future, that was destined forever to be a paltry village? The grid ensured that as much space as possible was utilised for building. This would be no city for the boulevardier, for the poet. It would be functional. It would have maximum focus on commerce. Every inch of it would serve a practical purpose.

Yet a 2007 report – 'Smart Cities: Rethinking the City Centre' – produced by the Queensland Government's Smart State Council, eerily echoed the tiffs and quarrels that fell about the city founders' surveyor maps almost two centuries ago. 'More worrying is the fact that there exists no plan for the centre of Brisbane, other than one for the CBD prepared in 2005 by the Brisbane City Council (albeit called Brisbane City Master Plan). Without such a plan, decisions can only be made on either a reactive or singular solution basis. There are some 30 precincts identified for major urban renewal within only 4 vicinities of the CBD, with no coordinated vision as to what is their combined sustainable capacity, how their dense working and residential populations will move around, nor what interrelationships might occur that could impact the city with a collective identity.'

Writer Rodney Hall, who would come to the city more than

a century after Robert Dixon's grid, said, 'You know, there's some strange thing that's happened in Brisbane in the way city planning has gone. It closes it in. I really kind of find it very oppressive the way Queen Street has got those covers over it. It's like everyone's frightened of the weather. It used to be such an open city. Now there are buildings leaning out over the street in Queen Street and I think of Grey Street in South Brisbane that used to have wide, wide pavements, a hot dust-blown street with houses set back from it, and now there's trees down the middle. It's all ... it's not a case of growing up and things look smaller, it actually is smaller. The space has been reduced. Brisbane's got one of the great climates in the world, if not the great climate in the world, and this idea of people being frightened of it ... well. The city was kind of haphazard; it was real and engaged with the place and the climate. It had a charm and a character. And I always thought Brisbane had very deep shadows. Dark edges and deep shadows.'

The progress of childhood, the boy thought later, was not unlike a Russian nesting doll in reverse. You started with the world in the centre – the kernel – and as you physically grew, and your consciousness expanded, you moved out to each larger doll.

When the boy stepped away from his miniature city of Brisbane under the house, walked out of the shadows and onto the hot white apron of the concrete driveway, he could see, left and right, the whole world of the next-sized doll, his suburban street. The street had a single dogleg at its lower northern end, and rose in the south where it hit a wall of bush and turned right. The bush blanketed the western rump of Mount Coot-tha.

He knew, to varying degrees, what went on in all of the houses in the street. At the hinge of the dogleg, for example, where the rubber tree roots had cracked the stormwater gutters, there lived an unhappy family, and sometimes he caught snatches of their arguments as he walked along the footpath to the bus stop. Opposite them, in a house that edged onto a small reserve with an enormous stand of bamboo, lived Mrs Black and her son, a teenager the boy was afraid of for no logical reason.

From north to south up the gentle gradient of the street, there was Mrs A and her husband and son. He knew that house. He often played downstairs with the son, enjoying a scale model railway set with a small engine that puffed real steam. He knew, too, that Mrs A had visits from a man named Mr X. Mr X always arrived after Mr A left for work in his little white *dak-dakk*ing Volkswagon. The boy once saw Mrs A standing alone in the front door frame of the house in a peach-coloured kimono. She seemed to be in a daydream. Did he know what he was seeing? What would a boy know of the human heart?

Across the road was the Murder House. It was made of burnt-orange brick and had a pitched tiled roof. The boy somehow knew, because nobody had ever told him directly, that a boy about his age and his father had been murdered inside that house. What did he know of murder? What was it? He knew that the boy and his father had been killed by the mother, and that she had slashed their throats in the night. He believed it was winter and he guessed the boy and his father wore striped flannelette pyjamas just like he did, and that the blood would have soaked deep into the flannelette. He knew that the mother had then killed herself by eating cubes of rat poison. In the story that he had somehow learned, in the Murder House a transistor radio had yabbered for days on the kitchen ledge, and washing went stiff on the Hills Hoist out the back. The murders happened while his own parents were building the little 1960s colonial a few doors up. His mother would later tell the boy when she saw the television report of the murders, and footage of their future street, that they knew their concreter had kept his word that day because they saw the house slab finished on the black-and-white television. There was another boy in the Murder House now, who liked to kick his soccer ball incessantly against a brick wall. The soft *thwack* of the leather echoed from the Murder House, over and over, like some maddening timepiece. The boy never played with the soccer kid, never even entered the yard.

On the other side of the street was a house with a black dachshund. It was owned by the fastidious Mrs B, who lived in the house with her mother. There was a caravan permanently parked in the backyard. The boy thought, for some reason, that Mr B lived in the caravan.

On the southern side of the colonial was the lovely, grandmotherly Mrs C, and her bespectacled spinster daughter Miss D. Directly to the north of the colonial was Mr and Mrs E. Mrs E trimmed their front lawn with scissors, and used the same instrument to puncture the boy's plastic footballs when they wafted into the yard. Mrs E called the police to complain about the smoke from his father's burn-offs in the corner of the backyard.

Mrs E, over the years, became very well acquainted with the local police.

Directly across the street was the boy's best friend, M. They had a special, secret, bird-like call to check if one or the other were in the vicinity and ready for play. They rode bikes, built shelters, formed their own exclusive clubs with hand-drawn merit badges, ran and wrestled, and hiked into the creepy bushland of Mount Coot-tha where one day, going further and to an altitude greater than they had ever ventured before, they found a concrete silo they believed was an air raid shelter from the war.

They knew every nook, cranny, crevice, bitumen crumble, ant nest, drain, emergency exit, fence hole, shade pool, dip, trough, hiding place, tunnel, tap, loose brick, rusted nail in that street; every rubber plant, cactus, jacaranda, poinciana, poinsettia, honeysuckle, elephant ear, gum tree and bindi-eye patch; where to find lizards, penny turtles, ladybirds, grasshoppers, toads, bird's nests, stick insects and spiders; which sections of footpath, in the heat, were cooler on bare feet than others; what part of the gutters, in torrential rain, formed fast flumes or eddying pools.

For the boy, life was largely lived outside. To be called inside was the end of play, the end of the day.

His city was conducive to that. He lived five kilometres from city hall, yet he had gravelly scrub at his doorstep, and stands of bamboo tall as a ship's mast, and creeks that had their own music. His skin was constantly in contact with nature. He was sentient to the air on his face when he rode his bicycle fast; the peculiar joy of standing in a cool pool of rainwater, formed in an instant during heavy rainfall; the feeling of the air tightening and falling still before a storm; the pleasure of peeling off sheets of sunburned skin; the rich smell of the nearby bush and how the perfume subtly changed with the time of year. He had pale scars on his face, elbows, hands, knees, ankles, and feet, from collisions with the earth.

Brisbane was tactile. There seemed no division between shelter and the open landscape. There was an impermanence about the houses, all matchstick and glass, especially where his grandparents lived closer to the city. Both sets of them lived in old Queenslanders. They were old, so it didn't surprise him.

But when the boy visited he knew the light fell a different way into these wooden houses on stumps. It was absorbed by the dark timber floorboards and glowed back just enough to show the shapes of things

— a piano, a sideboard, a figurine. They were shadowy, watery places, with some rooms lit like bright Chinese lanterns, and others permanently murky and sinister. They made noises when the sun jumped out from behind a cloud and hit the tin rooves. They whispered in a breeze and groaned as human weight moved around them. They were uneven. Window jambs slumped. Sections of the floor rose and sank. Doors didn't align with the catch.

At his nana's in Park Road, Kelvin Grove, the boy would stand on the back landing (the site, he knew, where his father in boyhood, as Superman, had launched himself off the railing for a quick flight over Brisbane, but instead landed feet first onto a steel rake concealed in the weeds) and study the remains of his father's old tree house in the backyard mango tree. The remaining beams were dark and rotted, and in some places the tree had actually grown around the narrow beams. He had seen this before, down in the Botanic Gardens, where a fig had ensnared an old park bench, the seat slowly and fatally enveloped by the tree itself, drawn into the trunk in a gesture that was both loving and terrifying to the boy.

At his grandmother's in Beck Street, Rosalie, he had played often in the old Buick with the flat tyres parked under the house, the leather seats cracked and issuing blooms of stuffing, the dials and lights dead, the view from all windows fixed forever. From the driver's seat he could see into the back-yard and the trunk of a giant poinciana tree, and littered about its base the brown, curved canoes of its seed pods. There were washing line props there, too. He often climbed the limbs of the poin-ciana tree, wrapped his arms and legs around the giant branches, and knew what it'd be like to ride an elephant. From the branches he could see his grandmother working the copper, not far from the Buick. Down one side, parallel to the Buick, was his deceased grandfather's workbench. It still carried an old rusted vice, and several tools and strips of wood. The boy could see Alice's house next door through a ragged and rusted fly screen above the bench, an old Queenslander which seemed to be collapsing into the earth itself, the creepers at the back crawling up over the roof, the guttering heavy with black mulch.

In Brisbane, the boy often thought, if you stood still long enough the vegetation would crawl up you, wrap you, and claim you back into the soil. The natural world was robust, even aggressive. Wasps and cockroaches were gigantic. The black pointy tips of the cactus plants always managed to reach out and strafe the skin, leaving behind a fine white line. Millions of bees hid in clover at certain times of year. Ant bites swelled the leg. Snakes slept near hot water systems. White ants devoured entire houses. Brush turkeys could move a ton of soil and gravel and bark chips halfway down a street to build their nests. Possums tore at each other in the night. Bats crashed into trees with great, wet explosive thuds, and by morning left a ground cover of decimated baby mangoes. Brisbane wildlife was arrogant. You were an undesired intrusion.

No, nothing was permanent in Brisbane, except the big and heavy Treasury Building in town, and Customs House with its green copper-domed roof, and the cathedrals, and the old convict windmill – a dreary stone thumb of a thing that never went away – and the crumbling Commissariat Stores down on the river, and the meccano set that was the Story Bridge, and of course the splendid city hall with its lions and its little red beating heart on the top of the clock tower.

His grandfather George had died when he was still a baby. His grandmother's second husband Geoff died, too, just a decade after. His great-grandmother Mary died around the same time, in the 1970s. He went to her funeral, then the burial in the cemetery. While the adults stood about the grave, he wandered off, fascinated by the broken graves. He thought he saw the floral dress of a dead woman in the dark crack of a nearby grave. He would never forget the dress in the grave.

In Brisbane, nothing was permanent.

Almost four decades after that funeral I take my young son to the Toowong Cemetery to revisit the grave of my great-grandmother Mary, and that of my great-grandfather Denis, my great-uncle Dennis — who died in infancy — and my great-uncle Syd. I have not been in the cemetery since the day I saw the floral dress.

The Toowong Cemetery is not far from our house. It used to be on the outskirts of town, back in July 1875 when it was opened for business, but today it is a large, hilly, 250-acre necropolis bordered by expensive suburbs, major roads and flyovers. It holds 127 000 of the dead, including four of my blood relatives.

On this warm Saturday we drive through the stone gateway. I have an aerial photograph from the cemetery website. It shows a grid of grassy roads and gravesites. Shadows balloon off the crowns of trees. Mary's grave is there.

'What is this place, Dad?' my son asks.

'It's called a cemetery,' I say.

'What are those things?' he asks, pointing out the car window.

'They're graves. Headstones.'

'What are those?'

'That's where people have died,' I say, unclearly.

'Are they dead, Dad?'

'Yes,' I say.

There don't appear to be any other people in the cemetery. Beyond the jumble of headstones and through a thin veil of trees you can see the colourful traffic zooming about the cemetery's periphery. This ribbon of colour is in stark contrast to the dreary grey and cream stone we're passing through.

The lanes are poorly marked and I accidentally stumble upon section 7a.

'This it is,' I say.

'What are we here for, Dad?'

'This is very special,' I tell my boy. 'You're going to meet, for the first time, your great-great-grandmother. And your great-great-grandfather. Your relatives.'

'Why?'

'It's important,' I say, helping him out of the car.

'Why?'

It's unseasonably hot. I haven't packed any water or sun

cream or a hat for my son. I check the printed A4 map for the grave locations. I know the exact lane and plot numbers, but I can't find any logical mapping in section 7a. The lanes are numberless, as are the bulk of the grave sites. I decide to start from one end of 7a and walk methodically up and down the lanes.

'Let's go,' I say.

My boy is full of questions, and excited by the grave platforms and fallen, broken stones and crosses — perfect ledges for climbing and leaping off.

'This way,' I say. 'Be careful. Stay with me.'

One second he is behind me, the next he's dashed off between the graves, trailing a dead tree branch he's souvenired.

'Finn!' I call. 'Back here.'

I walk up and down the laneways and find nothing. My boy is getting hot and irritated. The graves are in horrible shape. There isn't a single grave with any sign that it has been visited by anyone, not just in months, but in years. This is how it goes, the forgetting. The children of the dead die, and then their children get old, until nobody remembers anymore.

'Finn!'

I cover the entire section and don't find Mary, or Denis, or Dennis, or Syd. I see plenty of lifted grave tops that could contain a floral dress. Could my relatives' graves have been ones damaged by time or vandals? Could their headstones — broken and useless and illegible — have been swept up and removed by council gardeners? Could I have missed them during the hour it took to traverse the section? I might have missed one or two, but all four? I am confused, and disappointed.

'Let's get back in the car,' I tell my son.

As we drive out, he says: 'Did we lose them, Dad?'

'Yes,' I say. 'We lost them.'

Buried just across the ridge from my relatives in the Toowong cemetery is Thomas Dowse. I am interested in Dowse because reading about early Brisbane has proven one thing — there were few chroniclers of the settlement's first years. Local journalist J.J. Knight, who compiled the excellent *In the Early Days: History and Incident of Pioneer Queensland* (1895), wrote 'what a pity 'tis more of the early settlers ... [did not] reduce a few of their experiences to paper'.

Yet there was Dowse, dubbed 'the Samuel Pepys of Brisbane'.

At 15, Dowse was presented to London's Central Criminal Court charged with stealing a coat, waistcoat, trousers, shirt and handkerchief from his mother Catherine. He was found guilty, sentenced to death, and subsequently sent to New South Wales on board the *Florentia*. He was pardoned in 1839, after serving eight years as a convict, and made his way up to Moreton Bay in 1842, when the convict settlement was opened to free settlement. On arrival he described the place as 'the abode of damn'd Spirits'.

Dowse was a jack-of-all-trades – an auctioneer, a landlord, a small businessman. He ran an auction mart in Queen Street, and there, amongst the shirts, books and live animals for sale, Dowse discussed with local citizens the issues of the day, including his loathing for the convict system and the need for Separation from New South Wales. Dowse had his nose in everything in this small community. He was a prolific diarist. After the *Moreton Bay Courier* was first published in the winter of 1846, he found it a ready platform for letters filled with his wit and gripes. And he would become the first Brisbane-based correspondent for the *Sydney Morning Herald*. He wrote under the by-line 'Old Tom'. His pieces are sharply observed, shot through in turn with everything from political commentary to historical vignettes, character sketches and tantalising gossip. On his death, it was written of him, 'With very scanty advantages of education, his natural intelligence stood him in good stead … [he was] a free and fluent writer on passing topics' and 'his interest in current events never lost its edge'.

He wrote in one of his 'Gossip' columns in the *Brisbane Courier* in 1870, 'If Old Tom has a particular weakness more prominent than any other, it is, I confess, love of gossip; but, mind ye, not that detestable Mother Grundy kind of gossip that sets friends and neighbours by the ears. No, no, Mr Editor, my gossip, like old wine, shall smack of the flavour of genuine goodness, and not taste of the dregs of disappointed malignance.'

In his *Brisbane Courier* series 'Old Times', Dowse recorded his recollections of the early years of the settlement. In part of the narrative, he literally establishes his point of view as 'the platform of the old mill' – the convict-built windmill on Wickham Terrace – from which he can survey the early settlement 'and look more attentively at its residents in the clearing'.

It's a nice device, the use of the windmill, built in the late 1820s under the watch of Captain Logan, to grind the wheat and maize for up to 1000 convicts. Situated on a largely windless ridge that overlooked the settlement, the river, and all the way to Moreton Bay, it gives Dowse's reportorial eye a panoramic view.

'Let us', he writes invitingly, 'observe a few of the leading characters who at that time occupied the very limited social circle of the premature settlement.'

He writes of J.C. Pearce, storekeeper, in 'those days of damper and salt beef', who was financially ruined by a foolhardy 'experiment to introduce steam communication between the settlement and the head of the navigation'. Next door to Pearce was the 'old trump' William Pickering, a businessman who 'felt how hard it was in a limited community to make a pile, or, in fact, make tucker'.

Then there was 'the corner'. Dowse explains: 'The "Corner" − the veritable corner that has so much to answer for in the dispensation of villainous drinks and questionable I.O.U.'s − comprised that portion of the old barracks forming the corner of Queen and Albert Streets... that corner was a caution, and I venture to say, at this distance of time, that there are many old hands now remaining who could tell some queer and funny things said and done by the various men who have from time to time taken up their quarters at the "lucky corner".' (An old photograph of the 'corner' *c.* 1872 proves Dowse correct – heavily bearded men in top hats lounge about a portico at the barracks, the intersection of streets just cut up dirt and horse manure. A place for human transaction, yes, but from the looks of it a dangerous sort of male transaction. Who knows what was hatched there? Today, the place where Queen and Albert streets cross is part of the city mall, and is still a place where louche characters, particularly young men, hang about near a takeaway burger joint, and the police are ever present.)

So on and on Dowse goes with his memories that swoop and dart and soar from the ground level to the clouds, from earthy detail to lyrical whimsy. Brisbane was a hard place. There was little, if any, entertainment. There was nothing of beauty. Dowse says at least they had the pretty river and the bay to admire. They had, too, Dowse's prose.

He did it tough as well. He was reportedly attacked by Aboriginals near Shorncliffe and received a head wound. His first wife was a heavy drinker. As he wrote in his diary, 'The vice of drinking intoxicating drinks still hangs to her, making herself and family truly wretched.' Dowse moved to 'Hillside', his new house in Milton, in 1850. When his first wife died he married Sarah

Ann Fairfax. Eventually he passed away in his Milton house in 1885.

'With him passes into oblivion a rich store of colonial experiences and reminiscences, which it could be wished could have been published', a newspaper obituary said.

He left behind a sheaf of handwritten memoirs and some pages of a novel, *Tom Chaseland — or the Adventures of a Colonial half-caste — a tale of old times.* They are held in the State Library of Queensland, across the river from Milton.

And just a short walk from our house, within sight of my son's preschool built atop a portion of the former Milton and Paddington cemetery, is an apartment complex called 'Iceworks'. Once upon a time it was, indeed, an actual iceworks, delivering blocks to the people of Brisbane since the 1920s. Ice must have been profitable in this steamy city at some point, but not as profitable as 21st-century real estate.

So they built Iceworks. It sports a terrific upstairs bar and restaurant. It is situated on the corner of Given Terrace and Dowse Street, named after Old Tom. Down below, at the side of the building facing Dowse Street, is a small space called the 'Dowse Bar'. It serves cocktails and beers to the fashionable rugby crowd (Suncorp Stadium is across the road) and youngsters of inner-city Paddington.

When I made the connection with Dowse, and perused the *Moreton Bay Courier* digitised archives, I found a short article published on September 29, 1855, headlined 'Teetotal Meeting'. It was a report of the Brisbane Teetotal Society's monthly gathering.

'Mr Thomas Dowse, the Secretary of the Society, next made a general statement of the progress of the society, and announced the pleasing fact that he had received an official notification from the Government Resident (Captain Wickham), to the effect that the Governor-General had been pleased to direct the reservation of two town allotments of land near the reservoir, for the erection of a Temperance Hall and Lodging House. Mr Dowse... expressed hope that no long time would elapse, ere the buildings were erected, and eligible for use.'

Today, the only significant memorial to Dowse is a cocktail bar.

One humid morning in late November, I meet Brisbane city council historian Brian Rough at the old windmill on Wickham Terrace.

The windmill – the second oldest building in Brisbane – has sat on its hill overlooking the settlement, then town, then metropolis, since it was built around 1828. It was built with convict labour to grind flour and maize for the colony. Besides, Sydney was getting tired of sending provisions north.

As it turns out, the mill has just received another of its renovations. Supporting timbers here; braces there. Being Queensland, it's a miracle it has survived for over 180 years.

The squat structure, stripped of the struts and sails that would give it definition as a windmill, that would restore its meaning, now hunkers on the ridge as just something, a mass of stones, that belongs to our 'past'. It only exists because it somehow negotiated the centuries intact. It only exists because it is 'old' in a place without many 'old' things.

As school children, just across the ridges to the north-west, we bit our tongues with concentration drawing it in our exercise books. At its circular base we sketched miserable convicts in chains and the red-coated soldiers overseeing them. We dented the paper with little pools of blood. This place, we always knew, was a cruel place. Its role as a mill was completely obscured by the death and destruction we were told had happened here.

Brian Rough is patiently waiting with the key. I do not tell him how much I have always wanted, since I was a kid, to see inside the old windmill. Just waiting for Brian to release the padlock, I am back inside my exercise books, tracing the black pencil to the tip of a bayonet, distending the convicts' mouths in agony, neatening the soldiers' epaulettes.

'Here we are,' he says, and we step into the cool base of the mill. 'I'll have to lock this behind us. If people see the door open, seriously, they'll want to rush in and take a look.'

It's very quiet inside the mill. The walls are whitewashed and conceal a base of hewn sandstone quarried at now-suburban Oxley, and the rest is a diminishing cylinder of local bricks made of clay from nearby York's Hollow, then a gully and Aboriginal campsite, and now the showgrounds near present-day Herston, not far from the city.

It has survived a repeated changing of owners, threats of demolition and even a lightning strike. Rough is full of praise for the convict craftsmen who put it together. 'The guys who did the base knew what they were doing,' he says. 'You'd be hard pressed to put a butter knife between the stones. It hasn't fallen down. It hasn't burnt down. It's solid.'

The trouble with the windmill was it was beset with functional problems from the very beginning. When the sails failed to find power (Andrew Petrie would later claim the original sails had been installed back to front) to turn the wooden cogs and wheels, a treadmill was introduced. Human horsepower was required, and Captain Logan had several hundred convicts at his disposal. Thus it went from architectural marvel in the raggedy colony to object of fear and loathing. One of the millers who'd supervised the construction – John Oseland – fled a matter of days after its completion when the windmill's problems became apparent, presumably fearing punishment. He was never seen again.

The tread was like a cylinder of revolving steps. At any given time sixteen men would be on it, says Rough, for several hours per session. It was akin to walking continually up a flight of stairs.

In 1836 a man called William Ross, claiming to be a former Moreton Bay convict, published a memoir in London called *The Fell Tyrant, or the Suffering Convict*. In it, Ross recollects the windmill and in particular the treadmill: 'The brutality used on this piece of machinery, is beyond the power of a human being to describe. The unfortunate men are continually falling from it apparently in a lifeless state. I recollect 2 men falling from it, through absolute fatigue and were killed... they were hurried into their graves, like those who died a natural death.'

In September 1829 a prisoner, Michael Collins, became entangled in the machinery and was killed. For the next decade it would continue to suffer malfunctions.

'Let's go up,' Rough says, and we begin negotiating the dark wooden spiral staircase at the windmill's core. 'Stick to the outer part of the stairs.'

On the wooden walls of the staircase are little scribbles of graffiti. *L. Ferrier. 8.7.62.* L. Ferrier is found elsewhere on the other floors. L.Ferrier had a need to leave his or her mark. There is *Dulcie Gould, 1926.* And *McPhie, May 8, 1916.* Some of the graffiti goes back to 1911, probably the last time the walls were whitewashed.

We arrive in the cramped top of the tower and I can't stop thinking about poor Merridio and Neugavil, two Aboriginals who, on July 3, 1841, were hanged from the windmill. They had been wrongly accused of the murder of the surveyor Granville Stapylton and his convict assistant William Tuck in 1840. Stapylton had been beheaded.

So the accused were returned to Moreton Bay, and the dysfunctional windmill was used as a gallows. The windmill, at that point, was partly dismantled, but as J.J. Knight wrote, '… the disused arms made convenient timber for a staging which for the purposes of the execution projected from the balcony.' Aboriginals had gathered in the clearing around the mill to witness the town's first hangings. 'A pole was run out from a window above, and to this was fastened the fatal rope. The blacks having been pinioned they were placed on the staging, and without much ceremony or regard for the depth of the drop were… launched into eternity amid the howls of an astonished and demonstrative mob of blackfellows who had assembled about the hill to see the sight.'

'Beautiful view,' says Brian. 'All the early panorama photographs of the city were taken right here.'

As with much of my own city's history I knew of these stories, like that of Merridio and Neugavil, as some sort of vague spot of colour at the edges of my memory. Merridio and Neugavil lived out there, on the horizon, with cane toads and tram sparks and Bic pens and Mr Squiggle and a one-eyed teddy bear called Billy, and all the other detritus of my Brisbane childhood — that strange landscape inside me that never went away and with which I co-existed. It was a place for children, and there I had swept Merridio and Neugavil. I had not even known their names then.

A stronger, richer, more detailed memory was that this place was haunted by the ghosts of the hanged men. This is how we choose to ignore true horror, with a child's ghost story. This is how we turn our backs on real history.

It is a beautiful view. It makes sense, when you're on top of it, why Logan chose to put his windmill here. It's a deceptively high vantage point. You can almost see the fields of wheat and maize spreading out down the hills to the creek that ran from Roma Street and across the city site. The carts of grain making their way up to the mill. The twinkling of lamplight at night near the commandant's residence in William Street. The fog gathering in Frog's Hollow along Albert Street in late winter. The sharp morning sun in summer setting fire to the fields by 5am. The smell of the river and the fruit groves and, if the wind's coming from the right direction, the brine of Moreton Bay.

Poor Merridio and Neugavil. Who would remember them, beyond a silly child's ghost story? The windmill had, at least in the instance of their deaths, performed one function perfectly. There was another. When the city grid was surveyed and laid out, the windmill was utilised as a trigono-metrical axis point.

A century and a half later, it was again planned as an axis for another major construction, this time the imposing Queensland Gallery of Modern Art in South Brisbane.

As heritage architect Louise Noble asks in her 2006 conference paper, 'Re-reading the City: Indigenous Geography and Colonial Space in the Australian City', what relevance does a deeper understanding of 'unspoken history' have for the present, in view of Indigenous issues gaining importance in the field of land development and redevelopment in Australia 'as a direct result of the introduction of Native Title legislation'?

She cites the example of the new Queens-land Gallery of Modern Art at Kurilpa Point in Brisbane. The building's architects had originally 'aligned one of the axes of the scheme on the his-toric windmill built by convict labour at the crest of Spring Hill'.

She added: 'Consultation with Indigenous lead-ers informed the architects that the windmill site was the location of the hanging of two Aboriginal men wrongly accused of the murder of the survey-ors Stapylton and Tuck … the decision to align the building in this fashion was questioned and later modified in order to respect the wishes of the local Indigenous community.'

One evening my wife and I are discussing our new neigh-bour. She lives directly behind us, across the forested gully, and has just returned to Australia from a protracted and successful life in London and South East Asia.

She has lived in the little Queenslander through the trees for two weeks.

'She came in today,' says my wife, 'to talk about cutting down the gum tree out the back.'

Cradled between two large limbs of the Chinese elm, the ghostly pale gum towers towards the sunlight and when it moves with the wind it chafes and creaks beautifully against the elm. The sound has stopped me inside the house on more than one occasion. It sounds like the creak of sailing ship rigging.

'The arborist told her the tree has to go,' my wife contin-ues. 'The arborist says it's half dead. That when it falls, it will fall on our house.'

We lament the loss of trees in our back gully which, when we bought the house, we named after our son. Finnigan's

Forest. In just four years it has been gradually denuded left and right. And now the ghostly gum is to go.

'She seems nice,' my wife says. 'She wants to keep planting natives in her garden. Anything that has to go she's prepared to replace. She wants to start a nursery along our fenceline. She said we could have anything we want. She even offered us the gum tree when it's cut down. For timber, or mulch.'

I feel sorry for the old tree, down here in the gully off Latrobe Terrace. It was probably here when our house block was auctioned, as part of the Paddington West estate sell-off staged on Saturday, November 22, 1884. Ours was Lot 34.

'Paddington West. On the Ground. Sale at 2 Sharp', the advertisement read. *'Simon Fraser & Son are favoured with instructions ... to sell by auction on the ground ... the whole of the Paddington West Estate ... consisting of a series of Beautiful Elevated Ridges.'*

On Monday, November 24, the Brisbane Courier *noted: 'Messrs. Fraser and son report that the sale of the Paddington West estate was a complete success ... every allotment was sold ... the company of genuine buyers was large.'*

We are two kilometres from the city. We have a family of kookaburras in Finnigan's Forest. We have twice attempted to proof the house against possums. We have brush turkeys nesting below the veranda windows. We have noisy miners, crows, bats. We have lizards under the house and geckos in the roof and living behind the framed prints on our walls. Ants that, given the right conditions, can blacken an entire wall with their industry.

My wife, born in Sydney and used to a wildlife-free urban environment, is constantly aghast at what passes under, through and over our Brisbane house.

But she has grown attached to the forest and the doomed gum tree.

'How does she find it here in Brisbane, our cosmopolitan neighbour?' I ask her.

'She said she'd only been in her house a few days when a neighbour anonymously complained to council about how she parked her car in the street,' says my wife. 'She couldn't believe it. She couldn't understand why the neighbour didn't just knock on her door and talk it over, rather than reporting her to some authority.'

'That's terrible,' I say. I remember our former neighbour, Christian, and his constant battle with anonymous reportings over his dogs. He had gotten down to his final warning, and one evening the dog catcher was due at any moment: Christian had to plead his case to keep his animals. He came over and begged me to corroborate his story about how well-behaved his pets were.

'Please,' he said, his face sheened with sweat. 'Otherwise I lose them.'

Shortly after, he was back with the council official, and

I presented a lengthy narrative supporting Bonnie and Riley, the two black Staffordshire terriers. 'They are excellent dogs,' I said in their defence. 'And not a spot of bother. We've never had a single instance of trouble out of Bonnie and Riley.' Christian, red-faced, stared at the ground as I spoke.

It seemed to work. Both animals were given a reprieve.

Now we had the new neighbour being reported for some silly municipal infraction. Was it something to do with just our street? Or was it Brisbane? Or just the suburban world? I recalled Brisbane-born comic writer Michaela McGuire's account of working for a Brisbane Federal MP, in her book, Apply Within, *and taking calls from local residents complaining to the member that they had rodents in the house and would he please do something about it.*

'She couldn't believe it,' my wife continued about the new neighbour. 'She said, "Why is Brisbane like an entire city populated by people who have never travelled?" That's what it felt like to her. A whole city of people who have never travelled.'

When the boy was twelve he declared that he would travel the world. He had the globe on his small bedside desk and his favourite book was an atlas.

Then, when his grandmother from Beck Street

gave him his dead grandfather's Box Brownie camera, he declared he would be a photographer, or at least take the Box Brownie on his travels around the world.

He had taken a photography class at school, and with some difficulty located some spools of Kodak film that would fit the Brownie. The boy loved the camera with its worn leather shoulder-strap carry case.

He took photographs of his friends and of animals and plants with the Brownie, and developed them himself in the darkroom at school. He particularly enjoyed when the images emerged on the photographic paper in the chemical trays. It was some sort of magic, seeing the ghostly images form on the sheets of paper.

One day he was at his grandmother's in Beck Street, exploring the Buick and the poinciana tree and his grandfather's abandoned workbench.

He also asked for the key to the small, tongue-and-grooved wooden darkroom under the house. His grandmother kept the key at the back of a kitchen draw. The key was large and had a heavy brass tag attached to it. The tag was engraved with the word 'DARKROOM'. Only years later did the boy wonder why his grandmother kept that cubicle of a room locked. There was nothing in it to steal. It was a dusty space with a small sink and tap, some shelves, and some ancient wires hanging from one side to the other like a little clothesline. It held nothing precious.

The boy liked going into the darkroom and closing the door behind him. It was pitch black in there, except for white hot cracks in the floorboards and little stars of light that pierced through near the ceiling boards, and the little slivers and stars of Brisbane light in that blackness made him feel like he was floating in space. He loved it in there. It was mysterious. It was a portal to someplace else, to the past inhabited by his grandfather who died when the boy was eight months old. He had stood in this stuffy room with the stars, and developed his spools of Kodak in the white fat-lipped sink, and pegged the prints up to dry on the miniature clothesline.

But why was it locked? He couldn't understand it then, but would later wonder if the darkroom was some sort of empty, abandoned museum to his grandfather. A small, dry, rectangular vessel of Brisbane air that had once been breathed by his grandmother's husband before he died. By locking it, she kept that air in. A part of him was always downstairs, safe and sound.

One day, during another of his excursions under the house, he took the key to the darkroom and opened the door wide. The light outside barely penetrated the space, afraid to go in, he thought. He stepped into the room and waited for his eyes to adjust. And whether it was because he had simply never noticed it before, or that at this most recent visit to the darkroom he was a fraction taller as a twelve-year-old boy, he saw a small cylindrical shape at the furthest corner of the top shelf. He reached up and put his hand through a spider's web before retrieving it.

He knew exactly what it was, despite the dust and web. It was a used roll of Box Brownie Kodak film.

Of course he took it to school for the next photography class with the intention of developing it. He knew how to develop Brownie film now.

On this day, though, he asked his friend Bill, also an enthusiastic amateur photographer, to develop it with him. So they both put the old roll through the chemicals, and prepared the paper, and got the developing dishes ready and poured out the chemicals from the large white plastic bottles.

When the roll was done the boy inspected

the amber frames of the film but couldn't make out what was in them. He saw what he thought were eyes and fingers and black mountain ranges and white skies. What had his grandfather photographed with the Brownie? The boy knew he raced motorcycles on a dirt track outside Brisbane and he had plenty of those pictures back home. He'd taken pictures of his dog, Bunty, and the boy's grandmother and mother. He took shots of his signwriting trucks.

The boy went ahead and made a single print. He stood over the tray and wiggled the picture in the chemicals. Bill stood behind him, looking over his shoulder.

And an image appeared. It was a woman lying on a bed in a room he vaguely recognised. It was a woman with her head and longish dark hair against a pillow propped up behind her, and in the centre foreground were the wavy ripples of a blanket, and in the woman's arms were two very small babies.

The room, he quickly realised, was his grandmother's. The woman was his mother. The babies were the boy himself and his twin sister.

The roll had sat on that darkroom shelf for more than twelve years. It was there when George died one day while visiting his sister in Scarborough. It was there when the boy and his mother and father moved into their own house on top of the giant eggs of granite. It had been there all along, in the dim corner of the top shelf. Then the boy had found it, and developed it for the first time, and saw himself just weeks after he was born.

'Who's that?' Bill asked, pointing at the picture.

'I think it's me,' the boy said.

To mark the 150th anniversary of Separation Day – when Queensland removed itself from the colony of New South Wales and conducted its own business – I wrote a magazine article about the event.

I wanted to place the reader in Brisbane in 1859, to explicate the long struggle for independence. This was a moment that literally changed Brisbane city forever. Separation must have been, at the most, just an ideological notion when it was finally granted by Queen Victoria. What could have changed in Brisbane Town the day after the signing of a document in London, half a world away? It was still the same frontier outpost. Horses still dropped their manure in Queen Street. The convict mill still stood on the hill dropping the time-ball. Thomas Dowse continued to handwrite his novel over in his home in Milton. The bullock team-drivers still got drunk and fought each other in South Brisbane.

But now they had an *idea*. They controlled their own destiny.

I wrote: 'They awoke on that cool morning of June 6, 1859, not knowing the mantle of history was about to be lowered upon them.

'Instead, it was just another Monday in the out-post of Brisbane, and before dawn the settlement would have already been ringing with hammer strikes from the blacksmith's anvil, the whine from Bill Pettigrew's steam sawmill on William Street carrying across to the south side of the river, the oil lamps outside the pubs in Queen Street still flickering, and the whole settlement shrouded in wood smoke.

'The town's 6000 residents, and further afield the northern colony's dispersed farmers and squat-ters and shepherds, had been waiting for this day for over a decade. Yet like everyone domiciled at the bottom of the world, the gap between an actual event and news of it reaching the wider populace was measured by the passage of sail ships and steamers – whole lagging blocks of weeks, or months, to learn of the present which, when it arrived, was already the past.

'Unbeknown to them, later that Monday evening at Buckingham Palace in faraway London, Queen Victoria would put her signature to a sequence of documents that would permit the formation of the new independent colony of Queensland, separated finally from New South Wales and its seat of legislative power 600 miles to the south. After years of endless debates and disappointments, Moreton Bay and all points north of the 28th parallel would be free. Free to govern; free to determine its own finances; free to shape its own future.

'There had been hints that Separation was imminent. Two months earlier, in the April 6 edition of the *Moreton Bay Courier*, a news item stated: "It is the general opinion that the Separation of Moreton Bay is close at hand." Yet the same article chastised the local inhabitants, recommending they "turn over a new leaf" if they wished to distinguish themselves as administrators of their own destinies. "Never was there one that did less for itself having a similar motive and cue for action", the newspaper scolded.

'But on this workaday Monday, as Brisbane town roused to life, there was no glittering residue of what was about to come. It was as it was yesterday, and as it would be the following day.

'Brisbane was a difficult environment in which to make a living. Squatters – particularly those on the Darling Downs – earned the district's money and held the power. Churches flourished, almost as an antidote to a place that visitors described as dull and dangerous. It was a magnet to speculators and ticket-of-leavers hoping for a fresh start. And it was, unsurprisingly, a hive of gossip.

'Still, you could have witnessed that Monday, as the blue dawn gave way to a pale winter yellow, dirt streets like Queen and George rutted with cartwheel tracks and dotted with hoof divots and the occasional tree stump, and perhaps caught a pleasing whiff, above that of human detritus, from Mr Fowles' nearby biscuit factory. The entire town centre was a close jumble of industry, government buildings, general stores, bakeries, butchers, inns and horse emporiums. Wharves and stores crammed the river's edge from Petrie's Bight (beneath the current Story Bridge) around to the Botanic Gardens at the foot of Edward Street. Further round, the two-storey Commissariat Store building, facing the river and South Brisbane, left no doubt that the settlement was a mere pinpoint on the map of Empire – the royal cipher of George IV overseeing Queens Wharf.

'You could have encountered bullock teams loading up for return trips up country, the men fuzzy headed and working slowly after a night out with visiting shearers, perhaps, blowing a season's clip on pale ale. (Settler and diarist, Tom Dowse, described this endemic carousing as "the ribaldry and orgies of dissolute teamsters".) Avoiding the watered and fed bovines resting in the dirt, your attention might have been caught by the latest imported goods at the Tea Emporium in Queen Street – French plums and figs in glass-stoppered bottles, pudding raisins or East India limes. Or you might have picked up some West Indian rum or Old Tom Gin from Mr Oliver's nearby Wine, Spirit and Grocery Stores. You'd have to take a punt to South Brisbane to see Mr Peterson for some fine colonial cheeses and hams, or venture down to Fortitude Valley for some choice cuts from Mr Skyring Jnr's new butcher shop (appropriately situated opposite the Lamb Inn).

'In town you might have bumped into prominent storekeeper, radical and Legislative Assembly member for Stanley Boroughs, John Richardson. A Separationist, Richardson was contesting the imminent election for the seat of Brisbane, and would undoubtedly have been keen to solicit your support. Just two days earlier on Saturday, June 4, the *Moreton Bay Courier* carried a stern notice in its pages: "Do Not Vote for a lawyer. Do not vote for a man who is by every interest tied up with Sydney, and whose interest would suffer if Moreton Bay progressed. Reserve your vote for a thorough SEP-ARATIONIST..." You might have caught a glimpse, too, of Theophilus P. Pugh, editor and printer, and admired his small but energetic frame. He was not nicknamed the "Industrious Flea" for nothing. In ordinary times, you might also have been lucky enough to meet old Dowse, a former convict and jack of all trades, who'd settled across the ridge at Milton. But on this historic Monday, he would have been at home, still mourning the death in late May of his only daughter, Elizabeth, aged 11.

'You may have wished to avoid the area around the intersection of Albert and Margaret streets, famously known as Frog's Hollow. As one early resident described it: "North was a large shallow swamp about one acre in area. After a thunder storm it would be a miniature lake. It was the receptacle of all the town refuse. Dead cats, fowls and dogs would lie putrefying in the sun. It was tenanted by myriads of bullfrogs. Their nightly concerts is beyond description…"

'For respite you could have ventured into the fledgling natural reserve on the eastern flank of Gardens Point and witnessed the 40-year-old, Scots-born superintendent Walter Hill, scratching about his allotted nine acres, attempting to resurrect the former convict grazing paddock with its scars from decades of feeding billygoats and sheep and cattle, into an Eden worthy of beloved Queen Victoria herself. Just the year before, he had begun an ambitious project — the planting of his avenue of bunya pines, from south to north — and in his mind's eye, as he pushed his hands into the dry soil, probably saw them tall and creaking in the breezes off the river. He may, too, have deliberately turned his back more often than he needed on the eyesore across the river — the Kangaroo Point cliffs gouged for their porphyry or Brisbane Tuff for the town's hardier buildings.

'That Monday passed into night, and on Wednesday the local *Courier* advised that no "communication whatever on the point" of Separation had been received by officials in the last mail.

'What difference did another day make? A month? The Gayndah races were coming up. And

Dr Fullerton was giving a lecture at the Brisbane School of Arts on the formation of the blood – "Ladies who wish rosy cheeks for themselves and children are particularly invited to attend."

'In truth, many of the residents of Moreton Bay had grown tired of the Separation question. It had gone from a matter of urgency to a chimera. The debate since the infant days of the movement in the early 1850s had not changed – the Imperial and Colonial governments were indifferent to the people of Moreton Bay; capital directed to the port of Brisbane was "tardy"; labour was scarce; the northerners didn't feel amply represented by elected officials, being so far away from Sydney; the existing arrangement was a "melancholy and destructive farce". The locals described their burden as "a heavy clog".

'The Presbyterian clergyman, writer, politician, educationalist and agitator, the reverend John Dunmore Lang, became a champion for Separation having controversially delivered ships full of emigrants to Moreton Bay in 1848. A perennial opportunist, he founded numerous emigration societies and companies to facilitate his schemes for a robust Protestant working class in sunny Australia. Thus the *Fortitude* arrived in the bay without government approval, and the bureaucratic nonsense that followed just fired up Lang. He delivered lectures in Sydney in 1850 on the importance of self-rule for the Australian colonies, and wrote innumerable letters and articles to the colonial press on freeing up the districts and eradicating all the government red tape – in which Lang himself often became entangled.

'His fervour had its effect on many in Brisbane. On November 8, 1850, a public meeting was held to discuss petitioning the Queen for Separation. Another was held at Dowse's Auction Mart rooms in town early in 1851. This quickly became known down south as the "Moreton Bay Movement", and Sydney declared it doomed to failure. The northerners simply couldn't afford their own government. And once emigrants had tasted Sydney town, what could possibly induce them to head into the "Bush" that was Moreton Bay?

'Annual meetings continued. The "movement" formally became the "Moreton Bay and Northern Districts Separation Association". Gentlemen debated the issue back and forth at gatherings in the Old Barracks, the School of Arts, the Court House. In September 1857 the colony learned from British government dispatches – in the mail aboard the *Boomerang* – that Separation would finally become a reality. Secretary of State for the Colonies, Mr Henry Labouchere, announced that the British government, in principal, had agreed to Separation for Moreton Bay. In reality, a time worn bureaucratic process of ascertaining financial arrangements, the colony's constitutional make-up and its geographic borders, then began. In addition, changes of government in Britain shunted the Moreton Bay question back onto the waiting list. There were greater priorities across the broad canvas of the British Empire.

'But Brisbanites were rightly sceptical. They could not be truly free until the Letters Patent – establishing Queensland as a separate colony and signed by Queen Victoria herself – were published in the colony and proclaimed and read, along with the Queen's Commission, on Queensland soil, followed by the colony's first governor being sworn in.

'And so the waiting began. Rumours evaporated to nought. Candidates for the governorship were wrongly reported.

'Then on Sunday, July 10, a steamer from Sydney called the *Clarence* puffed its way up the Brisbane River towards the wharves, and was greeted with a 14-gun salute and "display of blue-lights", according to the *Courier*. Thousands of people rushed to greet it, "though they knew not why the salute was fired or the blue-lights and rockets displayed". The noise of the guns was enough to alert a sleepy town to extraordinary happenings. And "when the steamer neared the wharf SEP- ARATION was seen painted on her in large letters. Cheers announced the fact – the people rejoiced from their hearts." The mail confirmed that Queen Victoria had signed and dispatched the vital docu- ments, and a governor had been named.

'A general holiday was declared, and that week stores were closed and business suspended. Bris- banites took pleasure trips up the river and went on picnics. Cannons, firearms and fireworks were discharged. Police reported an atmosphere of good behaviour.

'And on Wednesday, July 20, the *Courier* bore a bold headline – "Advance Queensland". The correspondent wrote it would "be best to plunge at once into the news. The appointment of Sir George Bowen as Governor of Moreton Bay – now 'Queensland,' is fully confirmed." He and the Let- ters Patent were on their way. And their colony had a new name. (Not Cook's Land, as agitated for by Reverend Lang.)

'It had been a long time coming. Now the town had to prepare for the triumphant arrival of the governor in December. Ratty, uncivilised Brisbane had five months to turn over its new leaf.'

The governor took several months to get to his new fiefdom in distant Brisbane. He was due on Monday, December 5. In the interim, Brisbane fussed and fretted over how to suitably welcome Bowen and his wife, Lady Diamantina.

But in a letter to the *Courier*, dated September 28, 1859, 'A Working Man' wrote that not all the populace was excited about seeing the arrival of Bowen: 'As youngsters we generally have a mortal aversion to the individual who enjoys that title which is too intimately connected with the "cat-o'-nine-tails"... Pooh! Pooh! What a fuss about the Governor, a plain English gentleman, perhaps, who will only laugh at your gow gaw follies should you perpetrate them. First know him and then give him his triumph, should he be worthy of it.'

Bowen was late. His vessel, the H.M.S. *Cordelia*, under Captain Vernon, inched its way from Sydney up the east coast of Australia to Moreton Bay. The weather was reportedly poor. And unbeknown to almost everyone, Lady Diamantina was pregnant. It may explain Vernon's compassionate slow pace.

Still, the vessel arrived in Moreton Bay on December 9, and the couple were delivered to the city up the Brisbane River the following morning.

I wrote in my article: 'After finally coming ashore, the guns were fired and the party boarded a vice-regal carriage along with Robert Herbert, the new colonial secretary of Queensland (and soon to be Queensland's first premier), and Captain John Wickham, Moreton Bay's first police magistrate. The carriage slowly passed crowds of cheering locals waving the state's Separation flag.

'As the town had no official residence for the governor and his family, it was arranged that the Bowens would live in Dr William Hobbs' fine house – said to be Brisbane's best – built for him by Andrew Petrie, between today's Ann and Adelaide streets towards Fortitude Valley. The two-storey stone and lattice mansion had a broad view of Petrie's Bight and beyond to the bay, and a panoramic vista of Brisbane Town itself. (Government House proper, on the western ridge of the Botanic Gardens, would not be completed until May 1862.)

'The carriage was followed through town and by the time Bowen, his wife and the dignitaries had disembarked at Hobbs' mansion and made their way upstairs to the balconies facing the river, a massive crowd had gathered below on the steep grassy slope. On that balcony (today the house – the deanery of St John's Cathedral – still perches high up on a cutting above Adelaide Street, dwarfed by office buildings and apartment skyscrapers) Bowen took the oaths of office and Herbert read Queen Victoria's commission. Mr Abram Moriarty then read the proclamation of the Letters Patent (which had already been published in the first *Queensland Government Gazette*, dated December 10).

'The crowd roared. It was done. Queensland was born.'

In researching the article, I went to today's Government House on Fernberg Road in Rosalie, not far from my house, to view some famous documents. I had been there several times before, to witness the resignation of Premier Peter Beattie and the handing over of power to his successor, Anna Bligh. (By witness, I mean standing with the press corps on the impressive driveway below the front stairs of this white and candy-pink colonial building, in front of the azalea hedges.) I had also interviewed the former governor, now Governor-General of Australia, Quentin Bryce, in the front sitting room. I was generously given an hour, and we nattered about her life, beneath a framed section of a wool bale from Ilfracombe, western Queensland, where she grew up.

Of course Government House, which replaced as governor's residence the original house built for Bowen and Lady Diamantina overlooking Gardens Point, had featured right through my life. Beck Street was just below its spacious acreage, and my grandmother, I seem to recall, took some pleasure in living at the foot of something very British. This governor-and-commoner relationship was something she recognised inside of herself, from home. And although she was a cleaner for the well-to-do ladies of Brisbane's inner-west, and bought her clothes from an opportunity shop up on Latrobe Terrace, the tall, creamy quixotic tower of Government House, its regal gates, and its garden parties, were what she, as an Englishwoman, related to.

For the Separation story, I needed to see with my own eyes Queensland's founding documents. I knew Government House held the 'instructions' issued to Bowen by Queen Victoria – the oaths of office, the Queen's commission, and the Letters Patent that were declared that summer Saturday in 1859 from Dr Hobbs' city balcony.

The Letters Patent was probably the most significant document. A copy of it had been forwarded to Queensland for formal publication ahead of Bowen's arrival in August 1859. But where was the original, presumably carried to Brisbane by Bowen himself? An extensive search for it in the 1990s had proved fruitless. So an opinion was sought from Professor Glyn Davis, then Director-General of the Department of the Premier and Cabinet.

He wrote: 'The Letters Patent was issued by Queen Victoria under the provisions of an Imperial Act and was addressed to Sir George Ferguson Bowen (as an individual and not Governor of Queensland). The Letters, amongst other things, established the separate Colony of Queensland and appointed Bowen to be Governor. In other words, the original of the document was Bowen's Commission and, as such, Bowen was entitled to treat the document as his personal property. This is the situation with all Letters Patent – they are the property of the persons to whom they are addressed. This is undoubtedly what occurred and, if the document exists today, it is most likely contained in Bowen's papers.'

Was it a case, again, of Brisbane's, and Queensland's, collective historical amnesia? Did we care? This document was the constitutional basis for the state. But ultimately it was located in the UK's

National Archives.

As for the 'instructions', Bowen's family had gifted them to Queensland and they are held at Government House. Which is where I viewed them that winter day, at a table in a large, empty function room. The staff had retrieved them from a cabinet in the office. They were held in a simple plastic sleeve you could have purchased at any stationary store.

I was left alone with the thick 37-page document. The pages were stiff but in great condition. Before I finished taking notes, in a room with a view of bushland that ran down to a fence at the top of my grandmother's street, I gently slid a forefinger across Queen Victoria's actual signature.

Later, thinking about the arrival of Bowen – 'Pooh! Pooh!' as the 'Working Man' said in the *Courier* – made me think of the governor up on the hill in the big house, and my grandmother in its shadow, in a wooden worker's cottage held off the ground by stumps and joists that were salvaged from railway tracks. I thought of commandant and convict. Governor and subject. Parliamentarian and constituent. I thought of how, in this hilly city, the toffs always held the finest land on the ridges, and the workers sufficed with the gullies. The moneyed and powerful had views. The rest looked at each other in the hill folds. Even in Toowong Cemetery, the gentry have the high points, and the poor are interred in the gullies.

Is this Brisbane, or was it how any undulant city unfolded, across the world? Still, title seemed important in Brisbane. Connections. The school you went to, for some reason holds a certain power through life here. It has become a Brisbane cliché – the first thing Brisbane people ask you is 'What school did you go to?' – but there is a sliver of truth in it. There are innumerable powerful networks in this city that run invisibly across it like the old net of tram wires. There is not as much public brag-gadocio here as in Sydney and to a lesser extent Melbourne. Brisbane people, on the surface, don't necessarily celebrate the braggart, the flaunter of wealth, the famous face. But the networks are old, and run very deep.

I couldn't help but think that Brisbane's awe of authority, its casual acceptance of higher powers, its desire to quietly live by the rules, began when the pompous Bowen and his glittering wife set foot in Gardens Point. That at that moment – Separation Day — something else separated within the community too. It was the start of the haves and have-nots, the houses on the ridges and the cottages in the gullies, the garden parties and the quick smokes in the back garden, scratching away at life like the perennial brush turkeys.

Bowen was the embodiment of Empire. He made the laws. He symbolised the British gentleman. His manner, his eating habits, his foreign clothes, his reading tastes, his accent, even his gait would, I like to imagine, riffle out quietly and invisibly, and show the aspiring men and women of the city how it was done. He was the model for a future class in Brisbane, for divisions of class, when, before his arrival, the town had muddled along as a shabby frontier town.

Exactly 150 years after Bowen's arrival, on a steamy summer day in Brisbane, the first governor's landing and journey by horse and carriage to Dr Hobbs' house was recreated in the city. Bowen and Lady Diamantina (two acting students from a nearby drama college) once again stepped ashore at the bottom of Edward Street and were greeted by current Queensland Governor Penelope Wensley, Premier Anna Bligh, and a raft of officials. There was a jet flyover. At the 1859 ceremony there were

4000 people present, or roughly two-thirds of the population of Brisbane. At the 2009 ceremony there were 300 people present, or one six-thousandth of the population of Brisbane.

The Letters Patent were read in St John's Cathedral, next door to Hobbs' house and the famous balcony.

When I asked, in researching the magazine story, if we could stand on the actual balcony where Queensland was declared a state, the request was politely declined.

Nobody was allowed to step on the balcony. It was a workplace health and safety issue.

Two brush turkeys decided to make a nest beside the front of our house.

'This is lovely,' my wife says. 'They're going to have a family.'

My son watches with intense curiosity as, over the weeks, the turkeys — ugly, scraggly, gnarly-legged fowl — scrape together leaves and twigs with their powerful feet. The nest begins to take shape as a low, spherical bed of foliage. As the weeks go on it starts to gain height. That's when the turkeys move radially afield for their building materials.

About six weeks into the process we find ourselves hostage to their rampant grubbing and scratching. They cross the road and shift, with admirable patience, an enormous quantity of mulch from the neighbour's garden. They remove the soil from beneath our hedges. They flick out potting mix in pot plants. They scrape away the grass on the footpath in their mission to get more soil. Within two months they have decimated the garden. And into the nest they indiscriminately flick plastic food wrappers, a small broom handle, a small toy, cans and stones.

The mound is high now, almost level with the window louvers. The next-door neighbour, who is sharing the wonder of the nest with us, calls them her 'little hens'.

I give up tidying the front yard after them, chasing them, shooing them. I tie old CDs to string and hang them from the hedge and neighbouring trees. The turkeys are supposed to see their reflection and abandon the area, thinking the territory belongs to another turkey. Instead, our turkeys tear the CDs down and embed them in the nest.

I investigate hiring a turkey wrangler.

Then I wonder about my turkeys outside the window. If they are so territorial, could my turkeys be the descendants of the brush turkeys that Oxley must have encountered, indeed eaten, when he was foraging around the chain of ponds in 1824? Could I be looking at the relatives of the turkeys Oxley couldn't help but notice, flitting through the bush like ghosts, when the city was born?

I contact Brisbane's leading brush turkey expert Darryl Jones, Associate Professor and Deputy Director of the Environmental Futures Centre and Griffith School of Environment at Griffith University in the city.

He responds in an email: 'Brush-turkeys are primarily rainforest birds though they are obviously very flexible in their tolerance of changes. Even in undisturbed areas they tend to prefer the thickety edges and places currently overgrown with lantana appear to have been essential for the survival of the highly vulnerable hatchlings.

'So it is almost certain that the [rainforest] reported by Oxley would have been populated with the birds. However, being big and easily shot they soon disappeared and became both rare and shy, largely due to hunting.

'Nonetheless, they did persist locally (especially in the Mount Coot-tha area) and once they were protected in the early 1970s they started to reappear in places closest to their hide-outs such as The Gap, Kenmore, Chapel Hill, etc., and moved naturally down the vegetated creeks into lots of places where they are now common again.

'So it is not tooo much of a stretch to think that your current birds are relatives of the originals, though the intermediate generations had to survive the intervening years up in the bush somewhere.'

Of course the eggs finally hatch. For months the male

has been regulating the temperature inside the mound, and suddenly the infants — small balls of grey feather — are scampering throughout the garden.

Within days they're scratching at the undergrowth, kicking litter and mulch hither and thither. Within weeks they look like their parents with pinkish heads and blackening plumage.

Another generation of Oxley's children.

When I was a Brisbane expatriate, I looked back at the city as a place of childhood. And as childlike. To leave Brisbane — at least for some of us — was to leave your childhood.

Of course you can leave your childhood and stay in the one place while you're doing it. But Brisbane has a peculiar hold over its children, and some of us have to physically walk away from our pasts.

There are as many reasons for expatriatism as there are people. It could be political, personal, psychological. It could be to make a moral stand, or because of a lover's tiff.

But the Brisbane expatriate is different from that of, say, Sydney or Melbourne, London or New

York. No matter where they are, Brisbane people find each other, and can fill years with their grizzling and disparaging of their birthplace. I know of no city in Australia that produces such consistent bile as Brisbane does.

Conversely, Brisbane people I've known who strike out for the 'big smoke' want to impress to others, or perhaps just to themselves, that they no longer live in a hick town – and they then attract every cliché of their adopted city like iron filings to a magnet. They overcompensate. They tip too far the other way. They out-Sydney Sydneysiders in their rush to abandon a dull, ho-hum past. They hastily lacquer themselves with the cultural totems or tribal mannerisms of their new home, to the point where they stand out as ill-defined collages. They may even expunge Brisbane from their curriculum vitae altogether, or shrewdly hide it. Brisbane, as a spoken word, has little poetry, and comes off the tongue with more strine than our other capitals. *Brisbane*. I was probably one of these people, until the weight of wearing another city's clothes got too cumbersome.

To Brisbane expatriates, the city they left behind becomes blurred with all the things they saw themselves to be, and didn't like. It has no culture. It's just a country town. It has small ideas. The people are hicks. It's ugly. Boring. It's too slow.

And it is constantly described as 'a great city to bring up children'. I heard this when I lived away, and I have heard it repeatedly since I returned.

Former premier Peter Beattie told me one of his design priorities while in government was to ensure Brisbane became a liveable, family-oriented city.

He said when in government that he vividly remembered a child being killed by a vehicle on the Victoria Bridge that links South Brisbane with the CBD, and that he had kept that in mind when the Florence-inspired master plan of a series of pedestrian bridges across the river was being gestated. (He had a vision for several. Thus far, the Goodwill, Kurilpa, and Go Between bridges have been built.) It's hard to imagine another city in Australia where the accidental death of a child could ultimately influence multi-million dollar infrastructure.

As Kathryn Burns wrote in her University of Sydney thesis, 'This Other Eden: Exploring a Sense of Place in Twentieth-Century Reconstructions of Australian Childhoods', in 2006, 'Expatriate Queensland writers remember the warm climate and verdant fecundity through a veil of nostalgia, so that the region itself becomes associated with Eden and the timeless world of childhood.'

I loved my childhood, precisely because it was like being in a big country town, and it was boring to the point that you relied on your own resources to make it remarkable, and the ideas you had were your own, and it was slow, so slow that time barely moved, and you calculated when to go to school, when the lunch bell was about to ring, when you had to come in for dinner, by the colour of the light and length of shadows. I can't remember having my first watch until I was in my mid-teens.

When I came back to Brisbane the city had, in places, become unrecognisable. It was new and shiny. The people were positive and friendly. More than that, they had a spring in their step. Most of them didn't look like they were thinking of somewhere else, as they had looked to me in the mid-1980s on the eve of departure.

Brisbane-born people had chips on their shoulders. They had it when the settlement was treated by the colony of New South Wales as a useless village for hardened criminals. They had it as their toil and sweat in a tough part of the country was converted into income for the powers that be in Sydney. They had it when they separated from

New South Wales, and they had it in the 1980s after almost 20 years of state rule under the Kingaroy peanut farmer, Sir Johannes Bjelke-Petersen.

Joh became a national joke, and Queenslanders along with him. He and his hayseed colleagues continued Brisbane's perennial yoke to the colonial paradigm of rural wealth and power. Brisbane has always been a town with a whiff of cow and horse dung about it. And with Joh, a simple but cunning premier, it remained a big country town with the boss up in the Big House.

In 1873 the novelist Anthony Trollope, in his book *Australia and New Zealand*, had identified the power of the squattocracy, from the days of Queensland's first legislative assembly. Coupling this with what he saw as political apathy in the populace, it is little wonder the paradigm has been hard to shake in the Sunshine State.

'It cannot be said that this young colony has shown any tendency to run headlong into the tempting dangers of democracy,' Trollope wrote. 'It would appear that the prevailing feelings of the people lie altogether in another direction.

'As I have said, I fear more than once before, the squatters are the aristocracy of the country, and I found that a cabinet with seven members contained six squatters ... Among the working population outside the towns political feeling is not strong in any direction. Men care little about politics ... I am inclined to report as my opinion, that politics in Queensland are very quiet, whereas the loyalty to the Crown is very strong.'

As Australia changed and moved forward under Whitlam in the '70s, Queensland still had a country simpleton and environmental vandal in the chair, an authoritarian bigot from another century. A post-Separation squatter with a cabinet to match.

So the chip grew heavier under Joh. Queenslanders were cast as rednecked morons with a Bible on every bedside table. He was impulsive and go-to, and it was this that masked his appalling disregard for civil liberties, the environment, heritage, indigenous people and workers' rights. I remember from my boyhood and youth, the continual, simplistic assessment of Joh – 'At least he gets things done.' Over almost 20 years as leader he was distilled to convenient aphorisms best expressed with a match or grass stalk in the mouth, effectively screening him and his cronies from intellectual audit. Until along came Tony Fitzgerald, QC.

But Joh's famous personal and public measurement of progress and his success as premier was to count the cranes on the Brisbane skyline.

I met him once, by accident, in a hotel elevator when he was flogging his slender memoirs, *Don't You Worry About That!* (1990). In that mirrored cubicle, he seemed nothing more than a dotty old man. He appeared nervous and excited in the way that some old men can be when they interact with a world they no longer understand and find, to their surprise, that other people will still be polite to them, nod hello, register their existence.

He seemed utterly innocuous and harmless. Yet I had indirectly known the power of him, because he had shaped my home town and state in a way that had made my young self uncomfortable, and so I moved away. He had literally changed the direction of my life.

I would be back home, by chance, to report on his funeral in Kingaroy.

In 21st-century Brisbane, nothing seemed impossible, just as nothing was impossible to the city's residents after Separation in 1859 when, in a rush, and under their own rule, they hastily strove for a facsimile of Sydney or Melbourne or London.

That independence, that idea of managing their own affairs, had ignited Brisbane as soon as the fireworks for Governor Bowen and Lady Diamantina had faded and left their grey smoke smudge on the city skyline.

As I settled back in, I saw, too, that Brisbane people now had some sort of vague halo of confidence, the source of which I could not immediately identify. The state, of course, was going through a financial boom. It was resource-rich. There was money in town and you could feel it. Property prices were heading for the stratosphere. Brisbane, and Queensland, had turned its back on poor old Sydney and the crumbling, decaying financial state of New South Wales.

Peter Beattie was premier. He had a go-to demeanour as well as a folksy attraction – a can-do dynamism. He was smart. He'd travelled. He loved history and European cities. He wanted to see Brisbane criss-crossed by pedestrian bridges in the manner of Florence. He wanted to prove Queenslanders weren't a bunch of philistines *à la* the Joh era, so he built things like the massive and impressive Gallery of Modern Art on the Brisbane River to prove it – there, look at us now. He knew how to use and benefit from big, bold symbols.

Old friends recently visited from Sydney and were astonished at the city's 'newness'.

'It all seems so fresh,' one of them said. 'Like it was built yesterday.'

They had a toddler. They set him loose down at the Gallery of Modern Art, the State Library of Queensland, the theatre precinct, the city beach and children's rock pools at South Bank and marvelled at how he entertained himself there for hours, then days.

'It's a paradise for children,' the other said. 'How much are houses going for up here?'

The city looked and felt different, they said. There were funky bars down at New Farm and Fortitude Valley, gay pride marches, a cosmopolitan grunge at West End that held its own with Newtown in Sydney. It had designer-label clothing stores, fine restaurants, terrific cafes.

Admittedly they had not ventured into Brisbane's great suburban sprawl, but the heart of the city – well, it was beating.

On my morning runs beside the river, I heard every day the cyclists and joggers and walkers invariably talking about stock market figures and the property market and investments.

One day I happened to be jogging past an

elderly cyclist viciously abusing a young woman for wandering into the designated bicycle lane beside the river, not far from the CBD.

I told him to ease up, it was a beautiful day, just enjoy it. He pedalled up to me, got off his bike and pressed his face a few inches from mine, screaming obscenities. She was in the bike lane! He could have been injured. Etc.

I told him to go home, have a shower, and get ready for his job counting parking meter coins for the council. (Unkind of me, but seemingly necessary at the time.)

'Waddya mean?' he shouted. 'I don't have to work! I'm a multi! *A multi!*'

It reminded me of Sydney again. The whirl of money and property talk. The creeping interest in status. Brisbane was changing. Had it moved forward, or was it simply catching up with everyone else? Was this good or bad? I loved the new Brisbane, but I always wanted the place of my childhood too.

Then the boom ended, here along with the rest of the world. The city seemed a little less glossy.

And still, on the running track, they talked of investments and property and the stock market.

I never saw the *multi* again. Perhaps he and his

bicycle went down with the bust. Near the end of 2009 the state went from one of the boom states in Australia to a credit risk. The latest premier, Anna Bligh, even mooted selling off Queensland's assets to keep the place afloat.

Seemingly overnight, the serpentine river lost its sparkle.

In 2008 the Griffith Review *published an edition themed 'Hidden Queensland'. Editor Julianne Schultz pointed out that Australian Prime Minister Kevin Rudd and his Treasurer Wayne Swan were from Queensland (so too Governor-General Quentin Bryce). Rudd has a home in Brisbane, in a suburb on a quaint bend in the river to the city's east.*

Schultz wrote in the introduction to the issue: 'In the first half of 2007, when the prospect of a change of government was beginning to be taken seriously for the first time in many years, even close observers of the political process realised there were a lot of gaps in the knowledge they needed to make informed judgments. One well-connected insider took me aside and expressed his confusion: "It looks like these guys from Queensland could just win... I can see what they are doing, but I don't understand where they are coming from. What is their intellectual tradition? What are their formative influences? How do they think? I don't know any of this… if they were from Melbourne, or Sydney, or even Adelaide I would know this, but I haven't got a clue about these guys. Last time I looked Queensland was a foreign country, now look at them."'

And she would continue in an accompanying essay, 'Disruptive Influences': *'Australia's new political leaders are a product of a time and place that was uniquely volatile. This would be of no consequence except that this group of Queenslanders is now at the epicentre of national power. Understanding their motivations and where they come from as a group is significant. Now the rehearsal is over, the main game has begun and I see the legacy of a youth spent in turbulent times in their courage and their caution, in their desire for change and their fear of alienating powerful enemies, in their arrogance and their humility, their harshness and their humour and in their heartfelt desire to make a difference.'*

One of the finest paintings of the metropolis is *City of Brisbane* (1961) by Andrew Sibley.

Now held by the Toowoomba Regional Art Gallery (the painting won the *Toowoomba Chronicle* centenary art prize and was donated by the newspaper to the gallery), the picture is anchored in the centre by a rickety looking city hall clock tower and the great span of the hall's copper dome. One side of the clock tower is pale sandstone yellow, and an adjacent side is a menacing pitch-black. Fanning out from this centrepiece are dozens of red-roofed Queenslanders, the houses scattered willy-nilly, the patchwork they create pitching skyward in some sort of shabby suburban cairn. I don't see the river.

Sibley's Brisbane presents as some sort of Italian mountain village, the buildings jumbled and layered as they rise in steppes up the slope. It is chaotic. It's a little ramshackle. Houses, churches and old low-level office buildings are leaning this way and that. The entire edifice looks like it's about to collapse. Or be blown away.

I become fascinated with the painting because it's the Brisbane I was born into, before the arrival of Mayor Clem Jones, who has always been credited with 'modernising' the city, bringing CBD office towers and sewerage to the suburbs. It was all heat and mirages and shaded awnings with pools of shadow deep enough to disappear into and trams and men going to work in shorts and long socks. It was buckled roof-tin painted the colour of ox blood that, at some point near the end of its lifespan, came off on your fingers like powder. It was wooden house stilts capped with tin plates to stop the white ants. The white-ant tin was often frilled, to fit some notion of the aesthetics of the house. It was houses slumping at strange angles, the roof a different level to the floor line, door jambs crooked, windows sealed shut with subsidence. Sibley perfectly captures this slumping of the city, and looking at his painting you can almost hear nails pulling at wooden boards, and tin cracking in the heat.

Sibley, born in Sydney in 1933, was something of a prodigy. He travelled widely before settling for a few years in Brisbane, then home to the avant-garde painter Jon Molvig, who was to have an enormous influence on Sibley. They were friends. The young men partied hard and painted furiously.

Rodney Hall, living in Brisbane in the late 1950s and early 1960s, remembers seeing a painting by young Sibley on show in the city.

'It was very exciting,' says Hall on the phone. 'I first saw a painting of his in the *Courier-Mail* building when it was opposite the post office in Queen Street. It used to have a panel, a moveable panel that displayed paintings each week, different art works that they borrowed mostly from Brian Johnstone's gallery that was then the only commercial gallery in Brisbane. Anyway, I was in there one day on one of my breaks from work as a bicycle courier, and there was this fantastic painting, *Gothic Europe* I think it was called. [*Reflections on Europe* is in a similar stylistic vein to *City of Brisbane*, and was purchased by the Queensland Art Gallery in mid-1961. In August of that year it was displayed in the *Courier-Mail* Art Panel.] 'I thought it was a fantastic painting. When I got invited by Geoffrey Dutton's *Australian Letters* magazine to submit a sequence of poems for their series of poet–painter collaborations, Dutton's covering letter asked if I knew a painter I'd like to work with. I didn't know Andrew but I knew who I wanted to work with, and he lived in Brisbane, and I thought I'd find out from Brian Johnstone where he lived and go and call on him, which I did.'

Hall and Sibley became friends, and the writer would go on to write a small book about the painter. Sibley was then only 27 years old and was garnering serious attention. The man himself reportedly said of his time in Brisbane: 'I just seemed to paint and drink – a raw, desperate period – a struggle for survival.'

Hall remembers Sibley in Brisbane as vital and fascinating. 'He was such a great conversationalist,' he recalls. 'He was someone who alerted me to how colours operate. He said to me – "Look at these roof lines, the red roofs, with a deep blue sky and these roof lines, there's a kind of a shimmer along the top of all the roofs". He said it's because the colours are tonally balanced. If you saw them both as grey, it'd be the same grey, but there's this bright red and bright blue, and he was very interested and excited by the abutting of colours, the tonal balance of really vivid colours.'

Bulletin magazine writer Hugh Curnow first met Sibley in Brisbane, and wrote in a profile of the artist published on November 7, 1964: 'He was stretched naked and unconscious under a blanket on a mattress on the floor of what then passed for the nearest thing to an artist's garret in Brisbane: a tenement house in Petrie Terrace.'

The young expressionist was touted as the next big thing in Australian art before he was destroyed by the critics. *Sydney Morning Herald* art critic Wallace Thornton wrote that Sibley's paintings were rendered with 'a distortion that slips and slides in aimless, loose, decadent forms'. (There couldn't be a better description of *City of Brisbane*, and it's this very slipperiness that makes it such a brilliant and true picture of the city.)

In 1993 *Courier-Mail* art critic Sue Smith wrote

a retrospective on his career in reviewing a book on Sibley. 'His rise from 1960–62 was meteoric... just as quickly, by 1964 Sibley's dream run was over. When his art took a more serious, angst-ridden turn, it was savaged by the Sydney critics... Sibley withdrew to Melbourne, where he has lived ever since, and began the hard row back.'

I decide to contact Andrew Sibley and talk about the *City of Brisbane* painting. He is still in mourning for the loss of his wife Irena when I finally get in touch with him.

'Did you know my wife died?' he says sadly on the telephone from his home in Melbourne.

I ask him about the painting *City of Brisbane* and he says he doesn't remember it. I describe it to him on the phone and he asks me if I could send a photocopy of the picture to his home to jog his memory, and then we could discuss it properly.

I send his picture. Some weeks later he calls back.

'I remember I was on the highest point of Albert Street up from City Hall and I put up an easel and canvas on the footpath,' Sibley says. 'People walking by were watching me paint. The churches, the town hall, all those red rooves, I just put everything in. Everything was very red and copper-coloured. It's a bit of a mystery.' He once said one of the things he loved about Brisbane was that the city gave him 'more time to stand and stare' than other Australian capitals like Sydney or Melbourne.

Sibley, in the painting, has skewed the entire panorama, bringing in buildings that he couldn't have possibly seen from the vantage point of his easel, throwing other things out, gathering in the whole city from a single, narrow perspective. He crammed all of Brisbane onto that canvas.

I ask him why he didn't put the Brisbane River in the picture.

'I don't know,' he says. 'I lived in Petrie Terrace. All the hills. The red rooves.'

Some days later he telephones me unexpectedly.

'I did put the river in!' he says. 'Look at it again closely and you'll see a little piece of blue in there.'

He's perfectly correct. In the centre-left, a sharp twist of water.

'My wife died recently, you know,' he says sadly.

In our few discussions, painter Andrew Sibley mentioned on several occasions the address in Petrie Terrace where he had lived, overlooking the Roma Street rail yards at the eastern

end of the city.

I'd seen in a clips file a magazine article about his life in Petrie Terrace, when he was considered one of Australia's most promising young artists. Something prodded my memory so I retrieved the piece, published in Pix *on January 18, 1964, the year after Andrew had married his first wife, Andrea.*

'The Sibley's live in a two-storey Petrie Terrace home, which is old and picturesque,' the article reveals. 'Sibley uses part of the ground floor as his studio and upstairs are their living quarters. In Queensland, where one fireplace is far from standard equipment in a home, their home is unusual with 10 fireplaces for nine rooms.'

The magazine profile includes a photograph of a young and dashing Sibley leaning on the upstairs cast-iron balcony railing, staring out to the street beyond chiselled sandstone gates. The caption reads: 'Andrew and Andrea Sibley live in one of Brisbane's most picturesque terrace houses.'

The short marriage would end abruptly, and coincide with him suffering a nervous breakdown. As Sibley told journalist Hugh Curnow late that same year in the Bulletin: *'I married Andrea when she was 18. Now she's 19. She'll get over it. I think I have now.'*

By November 1964 Sibley had left Brisbane and was living in Sydney's Paddington, renting a house with a friend.

Nearly 45 years later, over and over in our conversations he kept returning to Petrie Terrace.

When I visited the old terraces, now overlooking the attractive Roma Street Parklands beyond the rail lines, I understood why the address kept insinuating itself with me.

My great-grandmother had once lived in this row of terraces, in its period of decline in the first half of the 20th century. My grandfather had spent several of his early years there. The family story was that they lived in relative poverty and rented a room to a lodger.

Long after, in the 1980s, one of the neighbouring terraces became a restaurant, and I recall a family dinner there to pay homage to our own connection with the place.

These same terraces had witnessed Sibley's most creative period, and the beginning of his youthful downfall.

One of the first novels using Brisbane city as its primary landscape was *The Curse and Its Cure* by Dr Thomas Pennington Lucas. It was published in 1894 in two volumes and printed by J.H. Reynolds of Elizabeth Street, the city.

The first volume was apocalyptically titled *The Ruins of Brisbane in the Year 2000.*

Who was Lucas? And had he really attempted a futuristic work of fiction set in my home town? What had ruined Brisbane that Lucas felt so compelled to warn us of, and in two volumes no less? Was he a seer? A futurist? An eccentric?

Once more I set off to find some answers.

He was, it turns out, an eminent doctor with broad interests ranging from mathematics to butterfly collecting. He was born near Edinburgh in 1843 to a Wesleyan minister father, Samuel Lucas, and mother Elizabeth Broadhurst. Young Thomas, it could be said, arrived in the world when faith and science were in collision. Reverend Samuel wrestled with God and Darwin and wrote three books on his intellectual dilemma. His son carried the identical gene.

In fact, Thomas took this interior debate a step further. He believed he had a mission to save humanity, after a brush with death as a teenager. He believed God had called him to a medical career. His father taught him homeopathy. He went on to practise in the slums of Lambeth, London – until his wife Mary died. He then lit out for Australia.

After spending some time in Victoria and writing copiously – he published everything from 'Do Thyself No Harm: A Lecture to Men' (which included the perils of masturbation) and natural history articles – Lucas sought the warm climes of Queensland, where he settled in Brisbane.

He set up his own practice and dispensary, and filled his home in South Brisbane with specimens of butterflies (including a previously unidentified example which was named after him). He applied for the position of Chief Entomologist at the Queensland Museum but was rejected after stoushes with local scientists.

In 1890 at the age of 47, after the deaths of his second wife and their two children, Lucas bought a 16-hectare farm in Acacia Ridge, 13 kilometres south of the CBD. He grew papaws in the belief that they contained remarkable medicinal properties and could cure a huge array of ailments, from constipation to preventing infections from, say, the removal of a bullet.

Then he wrote and published his dystopian two-volume novel, presumably out on the papaw farm, or when he had a spare moment at his medical practice.

One morning I went to the John Oxley Library in the State Library of Queensland and sat at a broad, empty table. The library precinct is not far from where Lucas first settled in Brisbane, on the river at South Brisbane. From my seat in the library I could look up and see the western rump of this city that would, according to Lucas, be in ruins by the year 2000. Wearing white gloves, I leafed through Lucas's crumbling book.

'In this volume endeavour is made to ferret out and explore those juggernauts of selfishness, which are crushing ... the people,' he wrote in his introduction to volume one. 'Brisbane is chosen as the ideal city. With local variations the story includes all the cities of civilisation.'

Chapter One opens with a man sailing towards Brisbane, up the river aboard his yacht, the *Lady Bertha*, in the year 2000.

'At first I believe I must be in Dreamland or Hades,' the yachtsman reflects. 'Everything is so desolate. No sign of cultivation meets the eye. No houses are to be seen.

'No mobs of cattle graze on the river's banks.' Lucas obviously saw a pastoral future for the city. 'Bush and forest hold extensive reign. Mangrove trees and bushes are rescuing mud-flats from the river in sheltered positions.' Still true today beneath the south-east freeway. 'Nature rules in primitive sway. If man ever discovered these shores, where is he today?'

Inexplicably, another sailing boat approaches our shocked wanderer. It is captained by Mr West and his beautiful young wife. They soon discuss lantana, and how it may now consume the former city.

How was the settlement destroyed? asks Mrs West.

'In the civil war,' the narrator answers. The 'battle of Lytton'.

Incredibly, the trio spot a Bengal tiger roaming the riverbank near where the up-market suburb of Hamilton had once been.

'Had you any Zoological Gardens in Brisbane?' asks Mrs West.

'Neither science nor art flourished in Brisbane, madam,' the narrator replies. 'Cash and bawbees, whiskey and cigars, is a descriptive gauge of Brisbane's ruling aspirations.'

Then they make contact with a man on the shore – Mr Greathead – who has apparently been granted 'the district of ancient Brisbane as a cattle run'. Through Greathead, they learn of the fate of the vain, inglorious city that lies in ruin at their feet.

'Half an hour's ride brought us to the brow of the hill, once the terraced boulevard of fashion and pride.

'The terrace itself was represented by irregularly scattered piles of broken bricks and mortar.

This was covered with lantana.'

The Treasury building (which I could see, bathed in rosy light, from my table in the John Oxley Library) was a 'heap of ruins', as were the former Legislative Houses at the bottom of George Street. There, the curious party discovered large snakes.

Lucas does not go lightly on his symbols. As if the snakes weren't enough, we learn the 'citizens of Brisbane have erected a Tower of Babel', and the tower has five foundation tiers – idolatry, uncleanness, drinking, gambling and smoking.

But what had caused the city to fall?

'I guess it was the land boom which swooned Queensland,' says Wilkinson, a friend of Greathead's and former minister of the crown.

'How did the land agents achieve such power?' asks the ever-curious Mrs West.

'The citizens hastened to get rich,' says the minister. 'The land agents saw the opportunity. They took it. Property holders were dazzled in elysian dreams. They entrusted their land into the care of agents for a boom, and the lands were boomed.'

Boomed land values – boomed house values. Such property values needed boom rents to pay the interest in the boomed capital.

Lucas concludes: 'The booms destroyed Queensland.'

Lucas brawled seemingly continuously with local doctors, politicians and businessmen. He had a public spat with government officials over a supposed outbreak of the Bubonic plague in the city. He was growing, or being shaped by his enemies as, a cantankerous quack. Lucas stood for the legislative assembly and hardly made an impression on the ballot. He started a company to promote his papaw products but had a falling out with other company executives and went broke. As World War One raged he published a bizarre book against German scientific culture, called *Dr Lucas' Papaw Treatment versus Kaiser Kulture*. You would think a tract on a Queensland fruit and its philosophical opposition to a world aggressor would hardly diminish his public image as a crackpot.

In Brisbane, under the sun, Lucas and his mission unravelled, and he died on November 15, 1917, a month after being declared bankrupt.

Each city produces its share of human oddities. But I wonder if Brisbane's colourful characters are any different from other cities. I wonder if a place that appears to be continually *promising* something – as it did to Lucas – can be even more detrimental than a damaged mind. Lucas, in his own way, was an intellectual with rigid beliefs and ideas. His opinions, and they were many, struck fierce opposition in Brisbane. They seem to have elicited an enmity in this small community, full as it probably was with little intellectual roosters pecking a niche for themselves in a young, naïve community, and perhaps it was this that finally brought Lucas down.

Yet he was ahead of his time. He was a champion of natural remedies over hasty surgery. He held strong Christian values. He was on a mission to save the world.

And Lucas was in many ways right about the boom destroying Queensland. He had a vision of greed and how it infects a modern city.

Not long after I went through his unusual novel in the library, my son badly skinned a knee out the front of the house, and after the initial wailing had retreated, and calm was restored, my wife sat with him for the moment of maternal cooing and medicinal treatment.

I poked my head into the bathroom as she was applying ointment from a red tube to the glowing graze.

I later checked that tube. I had never seen it. Or never noticed it.

It was T.P. Lucas's Papaw Ointment.

I telephoned Peter Beattie in Los Angeles where he was working as Queensland Trade Commissioner for the Americas following his resignation as premier in September 2007, and asked him what he thought of Brisbane city in the present time.

He said: 'Rebuilding the heart of Brisbane was a hard bloody slog. We [his government] had to fight for it every step of the way. Take the Goodwill Bridge. I'd been to Florence, and to make a liveable city you have to have pedestrian bridges. We had to fight the city council for that. The problem was we were surrounded by philistines. We never got any support when we were building the Gallery of Modern Art. There were no friends at home, you might say.

'When I left high school in Atherton and came to study in Brisbane, it was a big country town. It was awkward, like a gangly teenager. Now it's blossomed into a very beautiful woman that anyone would want to take out on a date. It was no longer embarrassing to have your friends visit.

'We're not philistines. We can appreciate art. We can read and write. We're not redneck morons anymore.'

Can I see anymore what I'm looking for in this quest to re-touch my childhood? To connect with another Brisbane that has surely disappeared?

When asked to write an article about the changing nature of the Australian childhood, I used it as a chance to continue my personal exploration of my city of the past.

For research, I went back to my old boy scout group at The Gap, a short walk from the house built above the granite boulders.

I wrote: 'I find myself standing rigidly to attention, head still, staring straight ahead, hands by my side like a toy soldier in the circle of 36 children, when Rama the Water Buffalo turns to me and whispers out the side of her mouth, "What name would you like?"

'I grin woodenly at the expectant children. They're all staring at me, issuing steamy little breaths on this winter night. I'm a stranger to the pack and I have to be accounted for. "I don't know," I tell Rama, perplexed.

'"How about Jellyfish?" she asks.

'"Yes, that's fine, Jellyfish, sure."

'"Cubs!" shouts Rama (or Wendy Hedemann, in the real world). "Tonight we have a guest, and his name is Jellyfish. Jellyfish was a cub here in the early 1970s."'

After more than thirty-five years, can I travel back in time, rummage through what's left of a period I remember as happy, innocent, and inextricable from the environment, and compare the relics to the shiny lives played out by today's hi-tech, time-poor, street-savvy urban children?

'"When Jellyfish was a cub, the den wasn't even *here*," Rama the Water Buffalo continues. "It was somewhere *else*."

'She is right, of course. Jellyfish's old den was a few streets east of this "new" den, itself officially opened a generation or so ago in 1974. Jellyfish's wooden den and its surrounding bushland have long been buried beneath the brick houses and pebbled driveways of Brisbane suburbia.

'Water Buffalo has unwittingly relegated me to museum artefact. Worse, I've been dated and linked to these young children's parents. Even worse, I'm a creaky marine invertebrate aimlessly lolling somewhere between their parents and their grandparents' era.

'Yet for a moment, standing with them in that circle, I am taken back — by the perfume of gum trees on a brisk, clear winter night in Brisbane; the names from Kipling's *Jungle Book* and the whole unchanged mythology surrounding these little cubs, especially the way they crouch in unison and touch the earth with the fore and middle finger of each hand; the leather scarf woggles with the metallic pin in the shape of the state of Queensland; and a voice in the back of my head, our Akela, our mother wolf, leading us in the cub mantra of dib dibbing and dob dobbing. Yes, Akela, we'll-do-our-best.

'Tonight's cubmaster, Baloo the Bear (Daniel Green), doesn't flinch before his charges. I'm as big as Baloo. I'm *older* than Baloo. So why am I feeling anxious here in this fellowship of good, decent, cheek- and ear-cold Lilliputians?

'I regret agreeing to Jellyfish. I wanted to be Hathi the Elephant or Keneu the Great War Eagle. I would have settled for Rikki-Tikki-Tavi the Mongoose. Why do I have to be some brainless bell-shaped sea creature made up of 98 per cent water?

'Yet Jellyfish it is.

'"WELCOME JELLYFISH!" the cubs shout in unison.

'And as their greeting echoes off the walls of gums, and the red antennae lights of the Mount Coot-tha television towers flicker warmly beyond the canopies of leaves, a pint-sized wag adds: "Jellyfish. Don't touch him!" The pack sniggers. Jellyfish stands there, smiling dumbly.

"'Later,' says the Water Buffalo, "Jellyfish will talk to us about what it was like being a cub at The Gap *all* those years ago."

"'Poor old Jellyfish,' I say, attempting a gag. Silence. Nothing. I flush to my hair roots. Instantly, I'm ten years old again.'

And later: 'At The Gap scout den Jellyfish stands in the shadows of a maelstrom of games being played under the stars. The cubs squeal their way through Capture the Flag, Blind Pirate and Frogs & Tadpoles before retreating to the den under the framed gaze of the Boy Scouts' founder, Sir Robert Baden-Powell, who watches on solemnly through cobwebbed roof beams holding up a forgotten home-made go-cart.

'I give my little speech, as promised. I tell the assembled cubs what it was like to be in their shoes *all* that time ago, and they listen attentively and give due respect to an old Jellyfish.

'In the end they rise, stand to attention, and one of the cubs says: "Thank you, Jellyfish, for talking to us. A big bravo for Jellyfish! Cubs! B-R-A-V-O!"'

'Looking down at them I know, somehow, that

the future of these children, together in the neon light of the scout den, is secure, and that what is happening to them here on this cold Tuesday night will be connected to their lives as adults. They just don't know it yet.'

I went back to my childhood street, and one sunny morning stood in front of the mighty, heaving ship of the bamboo. The scrub around it had gone, replaced by a manicured little park and playground with a cluster of generic swing sets. It was named after a prominent local member of The Gap, since deceased.

There were no children playing in the park, though it was school holidays. I went over to the bamboo and tentatively entered the dark amphitheatre. It was, naturally, a lot smaller than I remembered, but the carpet of leaves was there as always, and the music of the creaking.

On one thick stem of bamboo someone called Jimbo had inscribed his name for eternity. And on another, a creepy sign of the times: U R GAY AND U WANT IT... COME DOWN HERE. *Through the bamboo clumps I could see outside, to huge night security lights trained on the sacred grotto of my childhood.*

I walked up the street, impressed by the growth of foli-age, past the 'murder house' where, according to myth (or did it really happen?) a woman stabbed her husband and child to death with a carving knife, then killed herself with rat poison.

I searched for the vacant lot across the road from my old house, and the stump. But another house now stood there, and the stump was gone.

It was hard to know any longer what was real and what was invented, so I tracked down my childhood friend, Marco — now a happily married and loving father and still living in Brisbane, just a couple of suburbs away — to gain some clarity on matters.

'I remember us going down to the bamboo,' Marco said. 'It was always creaking. It was a place of real solitude. And kicking those plastic footballs that were really hard at either end and stung your toes . . . You started a club in the street and made badges and you had to do daring things like run through the prickle patch to earn a badge. We had a cubby on the vacant lot, under the tree, and we had a fireplace in there where we'd light up a fire even in the middle of a sweltering summer. The woman next door was always sticking a hose through the fence at us —

'Do you remember the secret call? It was like a giraffe with something stuck in its throat.'

'As kids we'd leave in the morning and not come home until dusk. There was that hot air balloon made out of gar- bage bags, with string and a piece of balsa wood at the bot-

tom and a soft drink bottle-lid full of kerosene. I lit it and it worked, it actually worked, and the balloon sailed into the sky and over the rooves of the houses. I thought it was going to burn down the suburb! It was a very good childhood when I think about it. It was very happy, and free.'

At the top of the street it was still possible to enter the bush beyond a line of new houses, and late on another morning I climbed a ragged path towards the summit. It was steeper than I remembered, the scrub thinner, and the hike was marked by discarded rubbish and the occasional ad hoc ramp built by daredevil cyclists. Near the top, over and around the huge heads of granite boulders (no doubt pitted with quartz and fool's gold) I came to a barbed-wire fence. The summit remained unreachable.

At that moment, my twin sister called me on my mobile phone. 'Why are you puffing?' she asked.

'I'm on the side of the mountain, above the old street,' I said. 'I'm trying to find what's left of our childhood.'

'You're there on your own?'

'Of course I'm on my own,' I said.

'You shouldn't do those sorts of things on your own,' she said. 'You could get murdered doing things like that.'

And on another occasion, a photographer preparing a body of work on writers and their childhoods asked to take my picture. 'Could we do the shoot in a place that means a lot to you?' I recommended we go to the bamboo.

After, as he and his assistant were packing their gear, an elderly woman walked her dog through the park. I had not seen her since the late 1960s, but I recognised her as Mrs Black, who lived in a house on the lower side of the street, nearest the bamboo.

I said hello to her and she was cheery and kind.

'You've been in this street a while?' I asked.

'Oh yes,' said Mrs Black. 'We've been here for more than forty years.'

'I lived up the road when I was a boy,' I said. 'I played in this bamboo all the time. You had a teenage son.'

She looked perplexed.

'Do you remember me?' I finally asked.

'Can't say I do,' she said, smiling.

By the 1920s, the venerable F.W.S. Cumbrae-Stewart and his wife Zina had become celebrities in small-town Brisbane. They were A-list – he with his intellectual credentials and she as a fearless social campaigner and charity worker.

Zina was also a keen investor. In 1913 she had purchased a large block of land with unrivalled views of the eastern aspect of the city, in Scott Street, Kangaroo Point.

And there it would sit, vacant, taking in the full sweep of the river as it coursed around Gardens Point, until 1925 when the 'Scott Street Flats' were constructed on the site. The flats, unique in the city at the time, were designed by architect Elina Mottram, a pioneer woman in the field. The two flats with seven rooms apiece were then rented out, while the Cumbrae-Stewarts lived nearby in Main Street.

So the couple had an expanding property port-folio. And she was busy, if not more frenetically paced than her husband. Described as an evangeli-cal Anglican, she held senior positions in innumer-able groups and charities, from the Queensland Red Cross Society to the National Council of Women and the Mothers' Union. She was outspoken.

In 1915, following a proposal by Queensland Minister for Works, Edward Theodore, for greater rights to domestic workers, Zina had weighed into the debate. At a meeting in the town hall called by the lady mayoress, the privileged ladies of Brisbane rallied to argue the issue.

As Jean Stewart points out in her book *Scrib-blers*, 'the most frequent talker was described by one reporter as "the staccato tongued Mrs Cumbrae-Stewart".' She apparently told the ladies that if servants were given more leisure the ladies of the house would have less time to execute charitable works.

Zina also caused a minor controversy in Brisbane when, during her presidential address for the Mothers' Union, she disparaged modern young women, criticising their attitudes and the way they dressed. She said boys should be given preferential treatment when it came to employment because girls could always secure 'occupations of housecraft, dressmaking and teaching'. She criticised young ladies' reading habits.

She gave endless public addresses, and was the first woman to speak from the podium in Brisbane's grand city hall.

So the arch-conservative F.W.S. and Zina were town gadflies, frequently in the press, darting from garden parties to annual general meetings to charity balls. He continued to lecture on Brisbane's past, fashioning himself as something of an expert city historian. And Zina, too, had a penchant for history. She would give a lecture on 'Brisbane of the Past' to the Brisbane Women's Club in 1933.

Manfred Cross, the former federal member for Brisbane and member of the Royal Queensland Historical Society, who's been interested in the

curiously placed Oxley obelisk since he was a
child, told me: 'F.W.S. was a celebrity. His wife was
a celebrity too. He would have been at all of the
garden parties at Government House. As the first
registrar and first librarian of the University of
Queensland he'd have been at all of the activities
associated with the university.'

On Saturday, September 27, 1924, F.W.S and
Zina strolled into the rooms of the Brisbane Wom-
en's Club in the city, for a celebration. It was the day
before the exact 100th anniversary of Oxley purport-
edly discovering the city. (How could the actual date
be celebrated, falling as it did on the Sabbath?)

F.W.S.'s written account of the festivities
went as follows: 'The President [F.W.S.] and Mrs
Cumbrae-Stewart entertained the members of the
Society, old residents and others ... for the purpose of commemorating the discovery of the site.
The President addressed the Society, basing his
remarks upon Mr Oxley's field books and identifying the spots where he landed, especially the place
at North Quay from which he saw "the chain of
ponds watering a fine valley," where the city has
since been built.'

Here it is at last. The error of fact that became
history. F.W.S. is unequivocal, before his small

audience, that Oxley landed at North Quay – *especially* the place at North Quay. This was a substantial shift in confidence from his *Queenslander* article just nine months earlier, where he wrote 'it would appear that he landed somewhere near the upper end of North Quay to look for water'. In the Brisbane Women's Club rooms, the historian spoke, and thus it came to be.

In attendance that day was none other than the society's patron, the governor of Queensland, Sir Matthew Nathan, the very man who, just seven months earlier, had made the first suggestions for an official obelisk to Oxley.

And a year almost to the day after this *faux pas*, Cumbrae-Stewart became one of the permanent trustees of the Oxley Centenary Fund.

So he had the facts as he saw them, he had the backing, and then he had the money and the power to put his historical error into granite.

Cross says he'd been perplexed by the obelisk – which he believed had been moved from the northern end of the William Jolly bridge, at some point, to its present resting place a few hundred metres further east, at North Quay – since he was a child.

'I could never understand how someone coming in a rowboat down the river ... well, anybody who looked at the height of where the obelisk is ... it's ten metres up the bank or something like that. Nobody in their right mind would come ashore there,' he said. 'Sir Raphael Cilento [former historical society president] said to me that Professor Cumbrae-Stewart was a very competent historian and he wouldn't have got it wrong.

'But he [F.W.S.] didn't study the Field Books carefully enough.'

I ask Cross if he thinks Cumbrae-Stewart, being fond of the first commandant, Captain Miller, had convinced himself that the 'chain of ponds' was indeed the swampy land at the bottom of Roma Street (current site of the Brisbane city hall), not Red Jacket Swamp and the surrounding waterholes in nearby Milton and Rosalie. Had Cumbrae-Stewart, blindly accepting Miller's choice for the city at North Quay, with another water source like Roma Street nearby, taken it as read that Oxley's and Miller's decisions were one and the same, and then worked backwards to shore up his argument?

'That's exactly right,' says Cross. 'I'm sure that's right. That's exactly the conclusion I came to a long time ago.'

So nothing stopped F.W.S. His obelisk was put in train, and it is a saga still shrouded in mystery.

For years my grandmother Freda had talked about 'that wonderful man' Manfred Cross, the young federal member for Brisbane in the 1960s. I vaguely remember her telling me that she had always voted Labor and for Cross, and at some point in the family narrative I got the impression she had actively campaigned for him during the federal elections.

There was also some suggestion that the benevolent Cross (it's only just occurred to me his surname could have a religious implication, for those so inclined, including my Baptist grandmother) helped in securing my grandfather George, sick with encroaching cancer, the last job of his career, as a messenger for the Queensland Law Courts in the city.

So when I'd contacted Cross to discuss his thoughts on the city, I proposed that we might have a long-lost connection.

My grandfather was George Baker, I tell him.

'The signwriter,' he says immediately. 'I knew him quite well. He did the ALP election signs when Ned Hanlon was a member.

'I can only say he [George] was a very obliging person. In those days Ithaca had the largest election signs I've ever recalled. We had signs that would be about five metres long and they were too damned hard ... they used to be stored under Len Eastman's house. They got cut down in size. Yes, I knew George.'

It shocks me to speak with a man I've never had words with before who has a picture of my late grandfather in his head.

I ask him if he ever got my grandfather a job, near the end of his life.

'I can't recall,' he says.

I have thought about that conversation now for months. It gave me a warm feeling, hearing that George was a very obliging person.

When I drove out to Kingaroy several days early to report on Joh Bjelke-Petersen's funeral, there were already no available hotel rooms in town, such was the clamor, so I ended up staying in a caravan park on the edge of town.

On the day of the event the mills were roasting peanuts. The service was to be held in the town hall in Glendon Street. Prime Minister John Howard, and virtually every living crony from Joh's days as premier, poured across the concrete apron and into the hall as crowds gathered behind ropes and security.

The service was held at 1pm. Kingaroy was at a standstill.

Later I wrote: 'At sunset they brought him home

to Bethany, past fields freshly ploughed and scattered with large round bales of peanut hay.'

Joh was interred on his property, beneath a stand of hoop pines.

I had already been several times to Bethany, outside town, to stand by the roadside and watch for anything interesting. There were always television news crews there. But on one occasion I was there alone, and was stunned to see a grubby yellow backhoe parked up near the main house.

This, I knew, was the machine that would dig the grave for old Joh. This would finally see him enter the earth.

I found something poignant in it. That this man who had been such a force in my home state, would now be buried with a piece of dirty farm machinery. A squatter to the end.

But there was another curious moment. As I watched the crowds file into the funeral – prime ministers, premiers, serving federal members, celebrities, sports stars, the notorious Deen Brothers who were employed to do Joh's late-night demolition of several Brisbane landmarks – I saw a face I hadn't laid eyes on in 20 years.

It was my uncle, an antiques dealer, and his wife, who had had a falling out with my parents.

I still have no idea why my uncle — a merchant in opals and stuffed eagles and old furniture — was invited to the funeral of Sir Johannes Bjelke-Petersen.

On January 1, 2010, the great Brisbane City Hall in the heart of town closed its doors for three years of repair and restoration.

It would be nice to think of this as a metaphor for Brisbane's present and future. That at a cost of $215 million, the Brisbane City Council was shutting the city's 'soul' in order to save it for future generations. That the council was showing its duty towards a cherished heritage building. That the restoration project was symbolic of how the council treasured the past.

This was not strictly true.

The building has been closed for major work because it had reached a point where it could have killed someone, or many people. It was a fire hazard and many of its concrete foundations were literally crumbling. It had been patched so many times since its opening in April 1930 that the remedies themselves — additional ceilings to staunch leaks, concrete floors on top of other concrete floors on the main auditorium balcony, to raise seating levels – had become dangerous. So the danger sparked the preservation of one of Brisbane's finest – and few – old buildings.

After Lord Mayor Campbell Newman first proposed the full extent of the restoration and a committee recommended immediate evacuation and work, a small poll of locals revealed that 40 per cent would be happy to see the building demolished (in a later poll this went down to about 20 per cent).

I was astonished to hear that one in four Brisbane people would be content with razing the building. Then I began to wonder if – with the city's incredible population growth – the 'new' Brisbane featured an increasing percentage of the populous with no grassroots attachment to the city, no history, no understanding of places like city hall and how it fitted into the city fabric and indeed the Brisbane narrative. Could it be that modern Brisbane – while focusing on becoming a new 'world city', and receiving waves of interstate and international citizens and simultaneously losing an older, entrenched generation to the ravages of time – was becoming a place without a memory? Is this what happens to cities in the 21st century? Was what I was feeling about this 'book without an index' just a reaction to contemporary global reality?

I recall interviewing former mayor and the so-called 'father' of modern Brisbane, Clem Jones, then 88, about a story I was writing on the first Ashes cricket Test ever played in Brisbane in 1928. It would be the debut test for a young man named Donald Bradman. It was held at the Brisbane Exhibition Ground, home to the annual agricultural show.

The English novelist, playwright and cricket *aficionado* Ben Travers had accompanied the English team, and many years later, in 1981, wrote a book – *94 Declared* – about his experiences. The team and Mr Travers stayed at the Bellevue Hotel (since demolished by the Deen Brothers) while they were in town.

Travers wrote that Brisbane in 1928 was still developing into 'the important modern city it has now become', a place where contemporary buildings 'contrasted with a colony of streets consisting of shack-like dwellings'. He said they could have come from a Hollywood Western.

The town was in a delirium over the match, of course. And on the second day of the Test, a little blond-haired 10-year-old boy, accompanied by his neighbour, spent the day at the Exhibition Ground. It was an experience he would never forget.

'It was wonderful,' said Clem. 'Tremendous. It was a hot day. I sat right against the rail on the western side of the ground.'

At the end of the day's play, little Clem, searching for a lavatory, then wandered accidentally into the players' dressing room where, he told me, he saw three cricketers physically fighting – English fast bowler Harold Larwood and two Australians.

'There were fists flying,' said Jones. 'I stood there for several minutes watching this.'

Whether these boyhood memories were accurate or otherwise, talking to Jones I realised I had traversed 80 years of Brisbane history and was speaking to an eyewitness to that famous Test. I was in the dressing room under the stands with Bradman and Douglas Jardine and Larwood. Clem Jones was grassroots Brisbane. Entrenched. He had, in his head, countless Brisbane stories that had passed into history.

And then a city loses people like him. And they lose those thousands of snapshots in an instant. A line into the past of the city is severed forever.

Jones passed away a year after I spoke with him, in December 2007. He had presided as mayor of

Brisbane for 14 years. His substantial seat of power was inside city hall. The city went from Hollywood Western set to a modern CBD, under him. He removed the city's famous tram system in favour of buses and car thoroughfares. (It's appropriate, in light of this, that the longest underground road tunnel of any Australian capital – Brisbane's 'Clem7' – was named after him.)

It was during his mayoralty, too – from 1961 to 1975 – that city hall began to suffer the aches and pains that would lead to its closure four decades later.

I recently toured the empty city hall to inspect the damage.

I had not been in any part of that building, except for the foyer, since I was a boy, performing on stage under the 4700-pipe Willis organ backdrop, in our annual school concert.

In fact I performed there in two school concerts. First as a 'hippie' complete with a wig, purple jeans, beads, and the T-shirt that my mother hand-stencilled: Peace Not War.

Then as Noah in a Biblical epic. I was swathed in

a scratchy sack, had a long grey beard and carried a staff. I would save the world from the Great Flood. Just a few months later, in January 1974, Brisbane would suffer its worst flood of the century, and I would be marooned in my grandmother's house in Beck Street, Rosalie, as the waters rose and rose up her front stairs and slowly but steadily submerged the huge frangipani tree in her front yard.

Now city hall – the 'people's place' – was shut. The perilous damage, accumulating over decades, had been caused by water. Water getting into the roof from day one, courtesy of a concrete slab covered in tar, *à la* the European method, yet catastrophic in the subtropical heat of Brisbane. And swampy water seeping up from below, washing away soil and flushing out poor-quality concrete. It took 80 years for the water to do its work and shut down the hall, entangling it in contemporary fire safety legislation.

It was closed just as the renovations to King George Square were completed. Now the statues of the old lions and King George V out the front of the hall stand guard over a largely treeless and bland city space that, in the middle of a summer day, is so glary that people don't so much walk through the square as shimmer across it.

At the rear of the new square is what resembles some bizarre, steel and concrete homage to the Queenslander veranda. The square itself is no longer flat: halfway across from Ann Street, it begins a long and gentle slope down to Adelaide Street. I can't work out whether this is for the benefit of pedestrians, or whether it is to subliminally discourage the citizenry from gathering *en masse*. On the other hand, in the square's surface are embedded hundreds of coloured strips of light that can flash in sequence. It reminds me of parties my parents held or attended in the 1960s, when people dressed up their homes with strings of coloured party globes. The dreary necklace of red, blue, green, yellow and orange orbs said — *this is where the fun is*.

I spoke with the mayor, Campbell 'Can Do' Newman, about the decision to fix the old building.

'There are so many different memories from so many incredible historical events at city hall,' he said. 'That's the thing about saving it. The older members of the community seem to have more regard for the issue.

'They've got more ownership of the issue because over the years they've seen so many things happen there.

'The thing about it is it's a lot of money and the

people who are a bit negative about it quite right-fully would be saying or thinking – and we don't get a lot of this – but every dollar spent in there is a dollar that could've been spent in my suburb, my local park, servicing my local street, doing up the kids' slides in the park or some other community service.

'But there is no other option. There's no "do nothing" or sweep it under the carpet. That's happened for too many years. It's time to bite the bullet.'

The mayor said he was surprised that the public had criticised his administration for its poor record on saving heritage buildings.

'It's interesting as well, there have been letters to the paper saying all the historic buildings are going in Brisbane. I firstly don't agree with that, but that phenomenon of loss of heritage committed in the '60s and '70s, well, in recent years there's been very little [of that].

'But surely city hall is important. If we're serious about saving these places it starts with the heart and soul of the city.'

I am given a tour of the building by senior council engineer Jim Mavronicholas. He agrees that the restoration is probably the largest of its kind in Australian history.

Then he tells me about the *Burra Charter*, the textbook on the conservation and management of buildings of cultural significance. The *Burra Charter* tells you how and how not to preserve the past. It talks of the *fabric* of a place, preserving the *fabric* in its existing state, not disturbing the *fabric*.

Indeed the fabric of city hall was altered, by then Lord Mayor Sallyanne Atkinson, in the 1980s. For decades the interior of the hall had been painted white. Sallyanne decided to bring in some colour.

'Now, come the late '80s, Sallyanne Atkinson decided she wanted to colour the place, she was sick of white,' said Mavronicholas. 'So she got all the painters in. All of a sudden it's all colours.

'All Greco-Roman structures are white. The shadows fall differently as the light changes. All of that is for you to appreciate on your own. The democratic ideology of the Greeks was, if it's all white, you decide whether you want to see this or that part of the building. You decided what you wanted to look at. To colour it changes the idea of the place. You're told what to look at.

'Now your paint bill is 40 times what it used to be. It absorbed a lot of the money that would have gone to resolving the engineering issues.'

What is most interesting is that the building, under the *Burra Charter*, must now be restored as Sallyanne had altered it, not returned to the original white. The colours have become the fabric of the place.

'The *Burra Charter* states you have to bring back the building to what it is, not what the builder built it as,' Mavronicholas added. 'People today remember it as a colourful place, with all this illumination. The *Burra Charter* will not let you go back to 1930. Nobody from that time is here now. Or has any context that is here now.

'People today remember the auditorium as being peach, and the library blue. It has *become* the colour.'

I telephone Atkinson and ask her why she decided to colour inside city hall. She replies, 'It wasn't really a case of tarting it up. I believe I was finishing it off in the manner it would've been finished if there had been more money at the time.'

I remember it as being white. I remember the great globes of light, on those school-concert evenings in the city – waiting in costume at the side doors in Ann Street, the traffic swishing by, the lights of my grand city fighting with the dying dusk, the terror I felt before going on stage tempered by the excitement of being in the city, at night, with all these lights that I had never seen before but which were on, each and every night, as I went to bed in the house built on top of the giant granite boulders . . . the different scents of the city, the shadows of people across the square, the footpaths gritty, the sandstone skirt of the city hall heavy and immoveable, the coloured clusters of people moving into the auditorium across the mosaic floors, the brilliance of families against the white walls, women in beehives and men in suits and thin ties, grandfathers in their best long socks and grandmothers who'd had their hair 'set' for the evening, the tones of amber and purple like strange clouds against the walls of white, a bus passing in Ann Street and riffling the hem of Noah's sack outfit as he waited on the street to be called to the stage with the Ark and the Animals, the darkness and then stepping into the white, the tall corridors and lights and polished floors saying this was an event, this was a moment to be remembered on this white canvas. And it was.

Writer Rodney Hall says this to me of the changes to city hall over the years: 'I think of the crime of what they did to

the square.

'*Albert Street went up a hill in front of city hall that, when you looked square onto the building, was sort of loz-enge-shaped, because the hill was sloping down: the stairs on the left-hand side were deeper and many more than the stairs on the right-hand side. There was then a triangle on which the building sat, visually, so that it looked like it was about to tip over, and it's such a mixed bag, that building, nobody else in the world would put a Venetian tower on a kind of neo-classical face like that. I mean it's just utterly bizarre.*

'*All the better because it is bizarre in my view. The palm trees stood out another three or four metres in front of the building, which gave it a very kind of graceful tropi-cal look. When they built that hideous car park [beneath the square] and flattened the square out, it took away the best art nouveau building in Australia, the old cinema, the Tivoli, straight across the road from city hall.*

'*The King George statue in the square, there was a dif-ference between the one they ordered and the one they got. They ordered this statue from a British sculptor and he sent them a maquette. When they got that they were very pleased with this equestrian statue, but the cost was more than they expected, so they ordered a three-quarters-sized version, which he delivered. But in the meantime he'd already delivered the two lions to flank the statue in the middle of the road.*

'They were full-sized and they'd already built the tall sandstone plinth to put the statue on. Then it arrived and it was too small but they still put it there and they put it there back to front, so King George had his face to the city hall and his horse's rump to the city itself.

'So there was this too-small statue on this handsome plinth with these great big lions and he was facing the wrong way. The city hall itself was this mixture of neo-classical and tropical and, you know, had this kind of spacious thing, and with its staircase had this visually undermining look to it, and all of it added up to a really, really exciting visual environment. It just, you know, it all worked in a way that it no longer does.

'I end up closing my eyes because I can still live in the city as it was.'

I speak with my mother's cousin, Allan Miles, who lived in Beck Street, Rosalie, next door to, then across the road from, my grandparents Freda and George.

Allan's father, Tom Miles, was Freda's brother. In their respective married lives, they and their two families lived as neighbours. I often wondered if this was the way it was with immigrant families.

Staying tight. Keeping close in a new environment.

Then I recalled my father's parents and grand-parents, just across a handful of ridges in Kelvin Grove. My grandfather's mother and bachelor brother both lived next door to him too.

I asked Allan to tell me what he remembered of my grandfather George, the motorcyclist and jack-of-all-trades, and what life was like in Brisbane in the '50s and '60s.

'My earliest recollections of Uncle George were when he lived next door to us at 125 Beck Street with Aunty Freda, Karen [my mother as a girl], and Bunty the bulldog', Allan tells me in an email. 'Upstairs in the lounge room was a large coloured painting of Lenin, and maybe another of a sec-ond personage of similar political persuasion. My dad tells me that I was frightened of the paint-ing. However, downstairs, "under the house" was far more interesting. That was where he [George] made his leather jackets and skid-lids for motor-bike riders, and also his photography and signwrit-ing workshop.

'In those days [*circa* 1950] colour photography was not for the masses, but George followed the common practice of applying colours to black-and-white photos. Not vivid reds and blues, but just a gentle wash of pale colours for the grass, the sky, a person's clothes and a few dabs for the eyes, lips, cheeks and hair.

'Uncle George would swear a lot. Every second word seemed to be "bloody" but I don't think he went beyond that, at least not in my earshot. However, if he was around at the church [the local Baptist church] he could eliminate the word entirely. I'm not sure that George ever actually "went to church" but he was sometimes on the premises for other events, and helped to build the new hall. On one such occasion he fell from the back of a truck while loading rubbish, and fell heavily onto his back. I don't know if this contributed to his death less than two years later [in 1962].

'Although George lived next door to us at number 125 and then across the road at number 120, I never really got close to him. If he was home he was busy at his work, or he was out on business-related matters or riding his motorbike. He had a gruff sort of personality that perhaps frightened me.

'George was one of the few men in the neighbourhood who were home most of the day. There were a couple of old-age pensioners, the mobile greengrocer with his horse and cart and the owners of the corner stores. George had his own names for some of the neighbours – Mrs No-neck, Mrs Rubberneck, etc.

'George was no gardener. Inside the back fence on Berry Street [that ran behind Beck Street] was a huge thicket of some type of tall weeds. Karen and Marion [his sister] and I used to play in it. As I recall, the back fence was sheets of corrugated iron, and not the usual wooden palings. That portion of Beck Street was unusual as the houses had a second frontage to Berry Street. Some of the neighbours in Berry Street did not like us referring to it as "the back street".

'The "other end" of Beck Street, east of Ellena Street, was somewhere we rarely ventured. It bypassed the local shops and the tram and bus stops, and had a nasty hill halfway along. However, we knew people from school or elsewhere who lived there. When coming home from town in a taxi, we had to tell the driver that we wanted the other end, or the "Government House end", as we sometimes pretentiously said.

'One governor, Sir Henry Abel-Smith, could sometimes be seen walking his dogs down Beck Street in the cool of the evening. We would say "Good evening, Sir Henry", and he would respond in a polite jolly old upper-class accent.'

In my tour of the closed city hall, engineer Jim Mavronicholas took me down to the basement and the home of the Australian Red Cross rooms.

I had been here as a child. It was once a tea and rest room for mothers who brought their young children into town for the day.

I was one of those children, and I have a memory, manufactured or otherwise, of alighting from a tram with my mother and sister and entering the staircase down into the cool rooms below street level.

It was there my mother decided to toilet train me, and I would not be going home with my family if I didn't use the lavatory rather than my trousers. Happily, I ended up travelling homeward on the tram that afternoon.

'I've been here,' I told Jim. 'When I was a boy.'

The rooms were seriously damaged in 2008 by subsidence of the soil beneath the building, and subsequently restored, before the full hall restoration.

During the restoration of the rooms, workers accidentally uncovered a wall covered in pencilled graffiti. As it transpired, the precious wall had once faced the urinal of the men's toilets and changing rooms. During World War II, the Red Cross rooms were used for enlistment.

'We found it digging under here,' said Mav-ronicholas. 'It's the most expensive thing we've got. Military details. Look at it. Rank and serial number. They went off to war and some of them didn't come back.

'Why is it all written in pencil? Over there was the counter where you used to get your hat, your pants, your shirt, a little notebook with a pencil in it. They were all armed with pencils.

'They changed into their uniforms here. This guy' – he points to a name – 'I've got his military record. I know where he lived up in Toowoomba. What farm he worked on. It's incredible, this record.

'We uncovered it by mistake when the painter was going to clean it and a little bit of plaster came off. All of a sudden this appeared. This was plastered over at some point by the council of the day. They plastered over it, maybe in the 1950s.'

There are 150 names on the wall, mostly privates from regional Queensland.

Mayor Newman reportedly said of the wall: 'The chance discovery of the historical wall is another reason we must save this heritage building.'

Chance discovery. Plastered over by council in the 1950s.

The book without an index.

I talk with Stewart Armstrong of the National Trust of Queensland about the rush of infrastructure development in the city — the freeways and traffic tunnels — as the state government and the Brisbane City Council try to cope with Brisbane's unceasing growth.

He says, 'The growth that Brisbane has seen in the last few years has been phenomenal, and the government's regional plan of creating growth areas around transport nodes is a great objective, but it's putting enormous pressure on the character housing of Brisbane.

'The Trust is still very concerned about this gradual erosion of Brisbane's character housing, bits and pieces disappearing for the new infrastructure and growth. If we're not careful Brisbane will become a city like any other; that iconic timber and tin house on stilts is just disappearing under development.'

One recent sweltering summer morning I headed down to the offices of the National Trust of Queensland, to discuss the sad stretch of riverbank that is – by error, mischief, insubordination or not – Brisbane's actual birthplace.

As I know now, the first commandant, Miller, had moved the temporary settlement against Oxley and Governor Brisbane's wishes – from Redcliffe to the current site of the city around May 1925. They came ashore not far from the Oxley obelisk site and set up camp around the present-day Queens Wharf Road and William Street.

I meet with Sue Finnigan and Dr Valerie Dennis. The Trust is housed in the former Immigration Depot, which was designed by colonial architect Chris Tiffin and opened in 1866. It is right next door to the old Commissariat Store, and we take a seat in a broad upstairs room that overlooks the site of Queens Wharf.

When the building was completed the great immigration push was on – post-Separation. Between 1860 and 1870, Queensland's population exploded from 28 000 to 115 000, and the bulk of those new arrivals first came here, for processing and lodgings. The men's sleeping and dining area was downstairs, the married couples' was the next floor up, and the single ladies' dormitories were on the top level.

Valerie and Sue tell me of the heartbreak and

disappointment that greeted many immigrants when they first arrived in Brisbane. There was little work, accommodation, or indeed food.

'My expectations regarding this colony have been sadly disappointed', wrote one migrant to an Edinburgh friend in 1867. 'It is cruel to mislead people by publishing imaginary accounts of the prosperity of the colony, and cause many to break up comfortable homes in the old country and come out here to be scorched under a tropical sun, as well as starved from want of work.'

Seeing this, I can't help but think of my grand-mother, Freda, a young woman who made the same journey as so many, less than 60 years after this letter was sent. 'I have hated every day of it since I stepped off the ship,' she'd said to me at the end of her life.

The depot was closed down in 1887, proscribed unfit for human habitation – a problem with river rats that still persists – and the Department of Agriculture moved in three years later.

'This was the minister's office,' says Sue, point-ing up to the metal-pressed ceilings. It's a miracle the building is still standing, earmarked as it was for demolition by the government in the 1990s – but then it was placed on the Queensland Heritage Register.

Sue and Valerie give me a brief tour of the men's dormitories downstairs, now filled with rows of computers and smartly dressed young men and women architects. We go into an adjoining space, dim and musty, and I'm told this was the shower and toilet facilities for the single male immigrants, and may have been used at one point as a morgue.

Then we head out the back of the building to Queens Wharf Road and the site of Miller's landing. There is nothing left of the two timber wharves that were built on the site by Miller and later administrations. Valerie says there was still evidence of old timbers there before the Riverside Expressway was constructed (its first section opened in 1973 in the time of Premier Johannes Bjelke-Petersen and Mayor Clem Jones).

The expressway literally traverses the western edge of the CBD above the riverbank. It does not intrude on Gardens Point or the North Bank precinct of the city, instead feeding traffic into the CBD via several off ramps. Planned not to impinge on city real estate, it obliterated the city's birthplace and put a curtain down on the riverbank, rendering it useless, dead.

Time and again this vitally historic precinct, with its weeds and crumbling roads and the surviving basement of what was once the city morgue, has defied definition. It has also evaded numerous attempts at redevelopment, as if, in the end, it is *too* hard to read, too far gone to enliven.

The most recent was the Beattie then Bligh government's $1.7 billion 'North Bank' super development, in the 2000s. The quixotic plans included buildings and floating wharves eating into the actual river space itself, a public square, restaurants, shops, a health club and even an Olympic-sized pool. It would consume the little John Oxley obelisk. Office buildings would rise up directly in front of the Commissariat Store.

The proposal prompted furious debate that stretched over years. Would it enhance Brisbane's historical precinct or destroy it? Could it revitalise a neglected stretch of the river? Or could Brisbane's famously fickle river endanger four 30-storey office towers built over its waters?

It was, again, another example of 'think big' Queensland.

As Doug Hall, former director of the Queensland Art Gallery, father of the Gallery of Modern Art, novelist and critic, wrote of this peculiar mindset in an essay on the city's newest bridge, Kurilpa, and the restoration of Old Government

House (once home to Governor George Bowen and Lady Diamantina): 'Brisbane has two new public projects that testify to its conditional relationship with history and its frequent flirtation with modern, public bombast.

'It's a city that likes to come of age. Depending on your point of view it can be anything from Joh-era cranes in the sky to the Commonwealth Games and the opening of the first stage of the Cultural Centre in 1982 ... it's a state of multiple comings, in fact. There's another recent nod to internationalism – a very large Ferris wheel at South Bank and it makes one think of great cities with Ferris wheels: that's the point, I guess.

'Is Brisbane so different from other cities? Sure it's a maverick place and there's much to admire. It's a city where parochial indulgence triumphs over critical reflection.

'But it's those self-congratulatory indulgences that many eschew, including life-long Queenslanders. Like the climate, the beaches and natural wonders – in celebrating them politicians speak as though it's of their own making – such is the manifestation of vulgar parochialism in a state that, metaphorically, shamelessly declares its dick is bigger than anyone else's. Perhaps finding exhilaration in imperfect expressions is one way to view it as a state of insecurity.'

I can't help but think North Bank would have fallen into this definition, if it hadn't been scuppered by public opinion.

So my thoughts come round again to the recent 'revitalisation' of King George Square, the apron in front of city hall. It yearns to be something else (perhaps Melbourne's Federation Square), and its grey bunkers – portals leading to public transport underneath the square – sit in the corners of the place like the abandoned fur coats of winter giants in a subtropical climate. Perfect for Berlin, not for Brisbane.

When this new square was unveiled, Brisbane people reacted with shock and horror. Not just Brisbane people, but the very civic administrators who'd presided over the design by Melbourne-based firm Urbis.

Former mayor Jim Soorley declared, 'It's a disgrace and an insult to Brisbane's most beautiful building. It's a blight on Brisbane and must come down.'

Councillor Hinchcliffe told journalist Des Houghton at the *Courier-Mail* that, yes, the scheme was approved by both Liberal and Labor members of civic cabinet, and yes, the plans had been on display for months. 'It looks like a bunker, it's very heavy,' he said. 'We were told it would be a light structure but I'm afraid it's anything but.' He told Houghton the portals seemed larger than they appeared on the plan.

Mayor Newman added, 'It's confronting in its raw state but it's not finished.' How could such a major piece of civic infrastructure be commissioned and built without – or so it seems – anyone actually looking and assessing the space as it was being assembled? Newman said the structures would not be torn down. 'It's too late,' he said. 'They are practically built.'

And this, it strikes me, underscores much of modern Brisbane's aesthetically jumbled CBD. By the time anyone decided to query or properly examine a project, it was too late – the venture had reached a point of no return.

Brisbane city itself has reached a tipping point in terms of the impact of its growing population. And now, after years of steady-as-she-goes, the state government and Brisbane City Council have abruptly embarked on a massive suite of road and tunnel projects that have turned much of the metropolis into a construction site. You can literally revisit a part of the inner-city after a gap of only a week and find that new bridge pilings and flyover infrastructure has been hoisted up in your absence.

Mayor Newman, a former military engineer, announced close to the start of his second term in 2008 that Brisbane was about to experience a protracted campaign of infrastructure to ease its growing pains. These included the Airport Link tunnel, the Clem7 tunnel, the Hale Street (renamed Go Between Bridge) link, a refurbishment of Kingsford Smith Drive, 500 new buses (he claimed bus patronage in 2004 was 48 million trips, jumping to 68 million in just four years), several more CityCat ferries and $100 million spent on bikeways.

In January 2010 Newman called for an urgent review into the planned chopping down of a 200-year-old tree on Lutwyche Road to clear the way for part of the Airport Link.

'They managed to save less significant trees for the Inner Northern Busway so I think this tree is worth saving,' trumpeted the mayor in the *Courier-Mail*. A concerned local citizen, Ian Ferrier, 64, said the crows ash tree was iconic to Brisbane history and had to be saved.

'It's pretty unusual to find something that large that's overseen the entire history of Brisbane,' he said.

Nine days later the tree was chopped down and removed.

Footage of the chain-sawing of the crow's ash was posted on a local news website. According to the *Courier-Mail*, 'It survived the floods of 1893 and 1974, thunderstorms that cut huge swathes through Brisbane, droughts and the scorching summer heat. But it couldn't survive progress.' It took seven hours to cut down and remove the tree.

The Airport Link construction company said nothing could be done to save it. The council was paid $100 000 in compensation by Airport Link for the tree's removal. The money was to go towards 'additional planting and landscaping for the community.' Relocation of the crows ash had been unfeasible, 'due to the risk to the tree's survival'. It was presumably better to cut it down than risk its survival.

A handful of residents had witnessed the tree's demise. It's 'a sad day', said one of them.

Brisbane. The city of points of no return.

Then when the boy's city went under water, he kept thinking back to the large wooden stage of the city hall just a few months before, where he had secured the future of the world as Noah in the school concert.

If this great flood had only been back then, at the beginning of the summer, he might have been able to help.

But he couldn't, because it rained and rained and Brisbane was in a permanent night–day fug of downpour and mist and humidity and there was no sun and the early morning neon lights of bakeries and the headlights of cars and the streetlights that never seemed to flicker off all caught in the thick ropes of storm water that rushed down the city gutters.

The boy had grown, and his family were, by then, living on a small property in a valley outside Brisbane, and that valley was crisscrossed by a few creeks and streams, and when the water came up it caught a lot of people by surprise, including the boy's family. He and his sister were stranded in Brisbane, at their grandmother's house near the chain of ponds, while his parents were caught by flash flooding and marooned in the little house in the valley.

The rains of the great flood didn't seem any different to ordinary old Brisbane rain. It was thick and it was heavy and sometimes if it caught you on a bare arm it bit the skin.

What was different about the rain while being trapped in Beck Street, near the chain of ponds, was the sound. Only at his grandmother's did the rain drum on a tin roof. He had no tin roof in his first house above the granite boulders, and none in the valley house.

But inside his grandmother's house the sound of the beating rain was so loud you couldn't hear the radio, or somebody speak. And this cacophony was joined by other tin-roofed houses in his grandmother's street, and then others in the surrounding streets, so that upon the broad concentric rings of wood and tin houses that pushed out from the core of the CBD, the rain was forcing a great symphony.

After some days the river rose, and it rose. Water pushed through where John Oxley had camped and taken notes about Red Jacket Swamp and the chain of ponds. It crept up Baroona Road, having flooded Gregory Park and submerged part of Milton State School, and it pressed on up Nash Street and began flowing up Beck Street.

The boy's parents had somehow gotten into the city by now, and were urging his grandmother to pack some belongings and evacuate the house. The actual street, the footpaths, the grass at the edge of the footpaths, his grandmother's front yard, the frangipani tree roots and trunk, the bottom stairs, were all submerged in the muddy flood water. The water continued to rise, moving up the front steps like a quiet monster.

Come, they urged his grandmother. You must get out.

There were men in bright raincoats puttering up and down the streets in motor boats. They sailed up to the residents' houses, warning them the waters were still rising. Come, they said, we don't know when the river will stop.

But the boy's grandmother was defiant. No, she had lived in this house most of her adult life and she would not leave. She had her cat and her budgerigar, and this was her home. Nothing, not even the hand of God, would take her from her home.

And still the waters rose, and the old Buick under the house went under, and the boy's late grandfather's photographic darkroom with its fat-lipped porcelain sink, and the old clothes copper, and the rusted laundry basket trolley; and the little fallen seed pods from poinsettia in the backyard floated about like tiny wooden canoes before the random currents took them towards the city or the waterbound forests of Government House.

I won't go, asserted his grandmother.

It frightened the boy because he kept thinking of the family legend of his great-grandmother, George's mother – Florence Eliza – whose life had been claimed by a Brisbane creek in the late 1950s. As the story went, she had argued with George the evening before her death, and disappeared. Her body was later found in the nearby silty creek. Police said she had drowned. The boy had seen the ivory necklace she had been wearing when her body was recovered, the mud still caked in the wrinkles of the necklace's carved elephants. The boy's grandmother *had* to leave before the great flood washed everything and everyone away.

Then, as the water crept even higher, in a flash she was being helped into a tin rescue dinghy, holding her green budgerigar's cage aloft, and its mirror bell sounded and the bird thrashed its wings and kicked up seed on the floor of the cage and tiny feathers tumbled – and this, the coddled suburban bird taken into a boat in the rain, was final proof that a great tragedy had befallen the city.

The water eventually receded, and for years the city talked about the great flood and the mud levels in houses and buildings and what had been lost. Every subsequent heavy rainfall or rise in the river was measured against this great flood. This was a flood city. The explorer John Oxley had seen debris caught high in trees, and other monstrous deluges had purged the city in the 1800s, and now it had happened again.

For a time, people in the city were brought face to face with the true, raw, brutal nature of the place. It had fierce heat that could crack concrete and bend railway lines and scald the feet. It had storms that could tear across the city in half an hour, and throw thousands of bolts of lightning at its citizens, then completely disappear, leaving a clear sky and streets and houses and cars enveloped in steam that rose and swirled from the earth just as it might gather at the top of a billycan just before the water boiled. It had vegetation that could push over brick walls and crack pipes and reach over structures like a suffocating hand. And it had a benign, dull, quiet, lazy brown river that inspired no poetry, yet could rise up just as nonchalantly and sweep everything and everyone away.

It was a place where you had to fight for your place, prepare yourself for, secure yourself against. It was a hard place despite the soft, effusive foliage.

A quiet place that could erupt in violent meteorological drama without notice. A safe place that could, in a second, turn extremely dangerous.

Everybody in the city knew this. Yet the heat – which has its own seasons and varieties of intensity – is like a narcotic, and it clouded memory, and it blunted alertness, and it returned everyone in the city to a gentle torpor, until the next catastrophe.

The boy felt, from the time of the great flood, that his city was now two things. It was everything that made his small, simple, and safe suburban world. Yet below all that, not as deep down as the great dinosaur eggs but close, pretty close to the grass runners and jacaranda roots and shattered fragments of brick and pipe, was a shifting, unpredictable strata of something. A membrane of impermanence.

Not long after the flood, the boy and his family moved back into the city, then just as quickly they left town for a new, less predictable life by the sea, an hour's drive to the south.

And he wondered, for a long time, if the flood hadn't caused this upheaval, loosened his family's foundations, cut them adrift and sent them away.

Rodney Hall was remembering Brisbane when he was a child. 'I have an anecdote I've many times told in public, but never written it down and published it. When I was a kid and we first moved into our house in Alderley, it was at the bottom of the hill. I awoke in the middle of the night and I could hear this roaring, I thought it was an earthquake or something. It was totally dark. There was a moon.

'What I saw at the top of the hill — the road vanished over the top of the hill, there were no trees or houses behind the top of the road — and what rose on the crown of the road was a silver pyramid, gradually floating upwards. And as it loomed, lit by moonlight, it became a house. And then it became the top of a truck with lights and two police motor-cycles. It came over the top of the hill and down the slope towards me. There was a house on the back of the truck.

'I used to have dreams that one day I'd wake up and all the houses will have been carted away — and if that happened in Brisbane in those days the land would have been seen to be unscarred . . . Far from having an underlay, there was always a sense in old Brisbane that it sat kindly on the land, that you could, if you were so moved, take it all away and everything would simply go back to the way it was.

'It had a kind of impermanence about it which is one of the things that has marked me totally. I wrote a lot about that in all sorts of fictional circumstances, the notion that there is impermanence to everything we have, and that's *something we should rejoice in. That was very much a part of my kind of feeling for Brisbane.'*

'Where did this city come from?' my son asks me.

Everything, to a four-year-old, has to come from somewhere. Even Brisbane.

'It grew,' I say.

'Like plants grows,' he says.

'That's right. It started off beside the river –'

'Plants need water.'

'Correct. And they had some convict barracks and a windmill and they planted crops so they'd have food to eat.'

'Did they have corn?'

'I suppose so.'

'I like corn.'

'Then more people started coming to the city in ships. People from the other side of the world. And they built houses and had families. The streets of the city were laid out and they made a few buildings from stone.'

'Where did they get the stone?' Because four-year-old boys seem to be very interested in rocks and stone and gems.

'They got a lot of it from Kangaroo Point, where we went the other day to see the new park on the river.'

'That . . . that was the place I wanted to see kangaroos but there weren't any.'

'Yes. Then when Queensland became a separate colony there was much excitement about the future and the people who lived in the city then made some very grand buildings, like buildings in Europe.'

'I know where that is.'

'They built a racecourse and had horse-drawn trams and theatres. And the city began to take shape, and more and more people arrived, and then they took large pieces of land and divided them into smaller blocks and houses were built in East Brisbane and over towards Milton and Paddington and Toowong in the west and South Brisbane – so the city grew from the centre and moved outward that way. In the city they built a great bridge across the river, the Victoria Bridge. First they made it from wood but the termites got it and it fell down, then they used stone and steel and then the floods got that one. There was a huge flood in 1893 and it almost washed the city away.'

'When I swim I can put my whole head under

the water,' my son said.

'Boats were stranded in the botanical gardens and people drowned and it was a terrible state of affairs,' I continued. 'So our city, like a lot of cities, has always had to make itself new again after things like floods.'

'Our house is old.'

'It is. It's about 90 years old. And there might have been another house on this land before our house. This little ravine we're in would have been part of a farm that would have stretched down from the ridge at Latrobe Terrace and all the way to the bottom of the little valley where the park is near Grandma's old house.'

'Can we go to the park?'

'There would have been cows and sheep grazing exactly where our house is. Anyway, the city kept growing and all the little housing estates joined up eventually and formed the suburbs. They go from Carseldine all the way north to past The Gap and Kenmore in the west and beyond Mount Gravatt in the south to Wynnum and Manly over by the bay. That's where two million people live.'

'A million trillion.'

'When Grandma came here on the boat from England they formed the Greater Brisbane Council, do you know what that is?'

'Nope.'

'That's when all the little councils and shires became one great big council, and that was really when the city started becoming a real city, with proper roads and trams and sewerage in houses and good water supplies. The whole city started coming together with the council. They worked in city hall.'

'Is that where the lions are?'

'Exactly. That's where the big bell rings.'

'I like them.'

'The lions?'

'Yes.'

'There were the two world wars. In the second war your grandfather George was an air raid warden. He took that job very seriously. They had to cover all the windows at night so that any enemy planes that came overhead didn't see the city down below. You know your grandfather was a painter. Well, he painted the shapes of tennis courts on the big gas tanks out near the mouth of the river, so the enemy, if they ever came, would think it was just tennis courts. That's interesting, isn't it?'

'Yep.'

'And the city was filled with American soldiers who came to fight the Japanese in the Pacific.

Brisbane was very important during the war. There was a thing called the Brisbane Line. That was the line that would be defended if Australia ever got invaded. Nobody would be allowed below that line. But it never happened. So Brisbane was a very different city during the war, with a great mix of people. One of your relatives went out with an American sailor, did you know that? We won't go into that. And one of those soldiers gave Grandad, my daddy, a special ring, but he lost it.'

'Can we go to the park?'

'It was a very interesting city then with lots of writers and painters, but in the end most of them went away to some place else.'

'Why did they go?'

'That's another long story, but the city wasn't enough for them and wasn't interested in their work so they went where they were appreciated. That happens everywhere, not just in this city.'

'I like painting.'

'I know. If you don't nurture something then it dies, and that's what happened to art and things in this city for a long time.'

'Like looking after plants.'

'Correct. Some cities are good for certain plants and some aren't. This is a very good city for sport.'

'We've been to Football World together.'

'But art is a little different. Though this city is changing. A lot of new people are coming here every week and with new people you get new ideas and new ways of seeing things. So we'll wait and see. What would you like to do now?'

'I'd like to go to Football World. Or do a painting. And can we go to the park?'

'Okay.'

On January 4, 1934, an eight-year-old girl published in the Courier-Mail, *Brisbane, a short poem. It was titled: 'At the Seaside'.*

> *Christopher Robin, hand in hand.*
> *Ran with his sister along the sand*
> *As on they ran, from close behind*
> *There came a bark.*
> *From big dog Spark.*
> *With big brown eyes and jolly face*
> *He chased them up and down the*
> *Place.*
> *Good dog Spark gave up the chase.*
> *And went home after his happy race.*

The author was Brisbane-born novelist Thea Astley. 'At the Seaside' was probably her first published work.

In the winter of 2004, at a writers' festival in northern New South Wales, I sat with Thea Astley under a massive Moreton Bay fig tree not far from the festival tents. She drank coffee and chain smoked and talked about Brisbane.

She had recently moved to Byron Bay to be closer to her son, and spoke of the town. She was frustrated that there was no public bench outside the town library where she went most days. She always arrived before the place was opened.

And she said she was tired. She'd had two strokes. Age, she said, was an annoying thing.

Astley was born and educated in Brisbane. Her father was a journalist. During the Second World War she was part of what was known as the 'Barjai' group. This was a gathering of 'cultural radicals', writers such as Barrett Reid, Vida Smith and later Judith Wright, along with painters such as Laurence Hope and Pamela Seeman. The 'Barjai' regularly met at the Lyceum Club rooms in Queen Street.

In our talk under the fig she returned again to Albert Street in the city and its shady history. The prostitutes. The gambling. She laughed as she remembered. She was attracted to the seedy side of Brisbane. She recalled the shabby corrugated-iron awnings that stretched over the footpaths.

Fittingly, she is memorialised in Albert Street as part of the Writers' Walk, a sequence of bronze plaques dedicated to Brisbane writers.

Her own plaque takes a passage from her novel, *A Descant for Gossips*: 'Queen Street and the trams blazed in at them, yellow and black in prisms of clanking light under the exploding overhead wires, the green and purple dust-ticklings at the tongues of the jolly-poles. The streets were half empty, and in the theatres the crowds sat jammed together in their unreal worlds, cuddling the dark and the fantasy of each other, and sucking toffees and shushing.'

We shared an unspoken camaraderie because we were both 'Brisbane' writers. We had been born there and we wrote about our city, albeit from the perspective of different generations.

In an interview in 1985 she had said of living in the Sunshine State: 'People are polarised very sharply into groups in Queensland. If you're a Labor voter, you're a communist! If you like trees, you're a hippie!

If you give blacks lifts in your car, you're a red! It's a difficult place to live because of the cut-and-dried attitudes. I think if you even like books you might be suspected of being a communist.'

Almost 20 years later she still seemed in good health. She was funny. She expressed surprise at finding herself in a place like Byron Bay. But it was precisely the sort of place, with its transient population and unending array of curious characters, she might write about.

After that meeting I went home and read her wonderful novel, *The Multiple Effects of Rainshadow*, based on a bizarre and tragic incident that occurred on the Aboriginal settlement at Palm Island, off Townsville, in 1930. In February of that year the island's superintendent, Robert Henry Curry, after a quarrel with the settlement doctor, went beserk. He blew up his own residence, incinerating his two children, Edna, 19, and Robert, 11. He also shot Dr C. Maitland Pattison and his wife. He set off from the island in a launch, cruised about for most of the day, then returned to Palm with two loaded revolvers. Curry was shot by a local Aboriginal man as he landed on the beach. The wounded Curry was taken to a boatshed and kept asking for his children. He died soon after.

Years later, a relative of mine, knowing I was inquiring into our family history and its relationship to Brisbane, sent me a photograph of a great-uncle – Alf Clausen – who at one time lived in Beck Street, near the chain of ponds. It showed Clausen as a young man on Palm Island, reading a copy of *Punch* magazine with two Aboriginal girls posed on either side of him. The girls were smoking cigars. Clausen smoked cigars.

'What was he doing there?' I asked.

'He worked there, as a builder,' my relative said. 'He was a very troublesome man. He liked to incite trouble between people. The story is that when he was on the island he started a great riot. There was some tragedy. He used to brag about it. He was proud that he was the instigator.'

'When was this?' I asked.

'In the early 1930s,' she said.

Could it be true? That someone in my family stalked Astley's novel of madness?

Just a few weeks after that wonderful hour under the fig, Thea Astley, great chronicler of Brisbane and Queensland, died. At the seaside.

Would Oxley ever be memorialised? It didn't seem so in the 1920s, as the granite obelisk was batted back and forth between departments within the Brisbane City Council, and its guardian, Cumbrae-Stewart, flitted to his social events, gave speeches, spoke on the wireless and wrote his historical newspaper columns.

In my search for the culprits behind the mis-placement of Oxley's plinth, I came across much interesting ephemera, not the least the spectacularly dreary languages that bureaucracies develop. The notes and memos that flurried within city council in the case of the obelisk sometimes took a year to be acted on, or a day if it came from the office of Mayor Jolly. The yellowing pages have their typed memo at their centre, but are busy with a cosmos of hand-written jottings, notations, questions and doodles in different inks and pencil scratchings from council underlings.

When Mayor Jolly finally allowed Cumbrae-Stewart to have his block of granite, the typed memo stating as much carries a craggy question in pencil — *what size*? And at the bottom a large sketch of the proposed monument, as dull and forgettable as it ultimately became.

Then on January 6, 1927, the town clerk sent

a memo to the city engineer. 'Professor Cumbrae Stewart states that the late Brisbane City Council promised as large a block of granite as could be obtained from the Council's Quarry for the purpose of making a Memorial on North Quay to Lieut. Oxley the discoverer of the Brisbane River.' He asked to be informed 'at your earliest convenience' when the block might be extracted and delivered to the trustees of the memorial.

Word got out within council. On January 13, Mayor Jolly asked the deputy city engineer, in a memo, to finalise the matter of the granite block. 'I would esteem it a favour ...' Jolly wrote.

The obelisk had entered the council bureaucracy, and Jolly's favour was expedited. On January 18, the stone was ready to go. 'One stone is ready, Soden's Ltd., have been instructed to cart it,' wrote the officious deputy city engineer in a report to the town clerk. 'Location of the stone is wanted, will some member of the Committee kindly let us know where we are to place it.'

Had a precise location for the obelisk been decided upon after years of negotiation? It is unclear. But it's interesting that council records reveal a persistent query to Cumbrae-Stewart – where do you want us to put the granite block?

By this stage Cumbrae-Stewart had all but driven the historical society into the ground, and now he was clinging onto the prestige – and the substantial public monies – of the Centenary Fund. It would get worse for both him and Zina.

Unexpectedly, the book without an index changes again.

I discover a death certificate for Ellen Miles. Ellen was the mother of Albert Miles, my great-grandfather, the diminutive tailor who brought his wife Kate and children – including my grandmother Freda – out from Reading in 1925 aboard the *Ormuz*.

I had always thought of Albert and Kate as the pioneers of our family in Brisbane. That's where the line – at least on one side of the family – started in this city. Brisbane was my story, my narrative, because of their contribution.

The death certificate states that Ellen Miles died on April 16, 1936, in Brisbane Hospital. Her occupation was described as *Home Duties*. She was 85 years old.

The 'Cause of Death' is shocking because of the multiple explanations. *Senility. Fractured neck.*

Right Femur. Pneumonia. Cardiac Failure.

The name and residence of the 'informant' on the certificate is 'Henry Fox, Son-in-law', of Isaac Street, Toowong.

And in column 11 – 'Where born and how long in Australia States, stating which' – it says: 'Amersham Bucksand Herts England', then '25 years Queensland'.

Twenty-five years? That would put Ellen Miles in the state in or about 1911. Why had Albert's mother come to Brisbane at least 14 years before he brought the rest of the family out?

The fact dissolves my long-held idea that Albert and Kate, with my grandmother and her siblings, had come to this place seeking a better life, striding forth on their own to a new city. The brave little rag-bag family from Reading starting afresh in a harsh, hot city at the bottom of the world.

No. Ellen had come first, and they had joined her in Brisbane because she was living in Brisbane. They had not sought out my city as a good place to start again. They had not independently weighed the evidence over in Reading – should it be Sydney, or Melbourne, or even New York or San Francisco? No, it'll be this place called Brisbane, because the family was already here. Does it matter that they weren't the family pioneers? Probably not. But it poses further questions.

I discover through talking further with relatives, that Albert's sister, Alice, had married a man named Harry Fox, and it was the Foxes who had decided to settle in Brisbane, bringing Ellen with them. Where was Ellen's husband, Thomas Miles? Had he died in England, prompting a widow's move to Australia with her daughter? Who was Harry Fox? Why did he move to Brisbane, bringing his bride, and mother-in-law?

Then I recall from my childhood a man named Ern Fox, who lived in a sprawling Queenslander up on Coopers Camp Road, not far from where I live with my family today. I have a picture of him in my memory, but am not sure if I ever met him. Had he been described to me as a child, or had I seen a photograph?

No wonder Freda hated the place, taken from probably small but at least secure council lodgings in Reading at nine, put on a ship for months, then landing in a little city in Australia, the light blinding, the heat like nothing she had ever experienced, the foliage huge and frightening, the electrical storms cracking over the ranges in summer, the houses wooden and creaking and dank underneath, the mosquitoes intolerable in this place of the ponds.

I look up Isaac Street, Toowong. There is no listing. But there is an Isaac Street in Red Hill. About six blocks from my house in Paddington. And newspapers from the early decades of the 20th century list an Isaac Street in both Auchenflower and Toowong.

Finally, the death certificate reveals one last thing. Column 9. 'When and where buried or cremated: 17 April, 1936. Toowong Cemetery.'

I had never known Ellen Miles had been resting over in Toowong all along.

In the 1970s when the boy was happily kicking a plastic rugby ball up and down his suburban street – evading imaginary combatants, driving behind invisible rucks, diving for tries, potting conversions between the posts from the sidelines – just a few kilometres away, in the city, a genuine battle was being waged on the streets.

In the winter of 1971 the Springbok Rugby Union team had arrived in Brisbane and were bussed to their fancy Tower Mill Motel on Wickham

Terrace. The motel was named after the city's famous convict windmill, just over the road.

Hundreds of anti-racist protestors were waiting for them, and more than 500 police were waiting for the protestors. It would be described years later by historian Raymond Evans as 'part of one of the most substantial and sustained anti-racist protests in Australian history'.

The boy knew nothing, tucked up in bed at The Gap.

The newish premier, Joh Bjelke-Petersen, had already placed Queensland under a State of Emergency for the team's tour. He seemed to have taken a leaf out of his predecessor Jack Pizzey's book with regard to public protest – Pizzey had creatively used the *Traffic Act* to quell anti-Vietnam War demonstrations in the late '60s. Then Pizzey died in office, handing the premiership to his Country Party deputy Bjelke-Petersen.

So it was Joh who single-handedly turned Queensland into a police state during the Springboks tour. The day before the team arrived, thousands of university students and academics had attempted to march from the University of Queensland at St Lucia to Roma Street in the city and on to Parliament House in the Gardens. In the city they were confronted by police, harassed, threatened and physically assaulted. Television news film was confiscated.

The 400 brave souls who gathered at the Tower Mill Motel, however, were to experience a violent confrontation with police that would go down in the city's history. Protestors were punched and bashed by hundreds of police. Some took refuge in the nearby Trades Hall, one of them the future Labor premier, Peter Beattie. He was beaten by police and taken to hospital.

Students continued to protest for days. The Springboks game went ahead at Brisbane's RNA Showgrounds oval, ringed by barbed wire and police.

Bjelke-Petersen would write in his memoirs *Don't You Worry About That!* (1990) that the Springboks 'emergency' was the first substantial issue 'on which I took a firm stand as Premier'. He said the position he adopted against the 1971 anti-Springbok demonstration 'put me on the map' politically throughout Australia. He reflected it was the inaugural moment when the Premier of Queensland was recognised as a person who 'could not be pushed around by militants acting outside the law'. Political commentators speculated it was the making of Bjelke-Petersen. The man himself concluded: 'I think it restored people's faith in the rule of law.'

The boy, fast asleep with his globe of the world motionless on his desk in the dark, didn't know either that his city had changed into something else that winter. It stopped moving forward. It was the capital of the police state. It was presided over by a peanut farmer from another era who had unwittingly turned the boy's hometown into a national joke. A joke that would persist for decades and infiltrate the city's consciousness and attack its confidence and self-esteem and return a chip to its shoulder that it probably hadn't had since the decade prior to Separation from New South Wales in 1859.

It would precipitate the intellectual and cultural drain from the city that would, in turn, perpetuate a reputation for backwardness and inertia.

Writer Rodney Hall was just one artist who fled the state.

'I was present at the arrival of the Springboks team, and the police were incredibly violent,' he remembers. 'And I just thought, I can't live here. This isn't a place where you're allowed to think for yourself. You either toed the line or else. It was no place to live.

'I'd organised what I thought was the most successful protest against the Springboks football team. Judith Wright and I got together and invited Kath Walker and pastor Doug Nicholls, an Aboriginal pastor who subsequently became governor of Victoria, and two friends of mine, Bill and Joan Carr – they were very stylish people, very independent-minded people.

'I'd booked a table for six in the motel where the Springboks were staying. They'd assembled a big table in the dining room and Judith and I turned up first and settled ourselves at the table. This was how we'd planned it, and our two other guests – Bill and his wife – were with us and we'd arranged for Kath and Doug, as black people, to arrive later, which they did. And we managed, by negotiation with the waiter who was settling us, to be settled nearby the tables where the Springboks were.

'When Kath and Doug came in we made a huge business of kissing them, you know, and hugging them and carrying on and sitting them down, making sure they faced the Springboks' table and they were served.

'And actually one of that team did lodge a complaint with the hotel staff. Apparently – we only found this out when we were leaving – the motel refused to acknowledge that anything was out of order at all. But the team had had an uncomfortable meal.

'We left the city because it was a police state – and whatever people say, it was. I had no other reason for moving, but we moved to Sydney and I found a job there and we never moved back to Brisbane.'

Lives were changing, the city was changing, as the boy slept, his rugby ball placed carefully at the end of the bed where he knew he could find it the next morning and sneak in a quick kick in the dew before school.

It had always been a city where radical public protest had occurred, and race riots, and political assassination attempts, and corruption, but some Brisbane people slept and some didn't.

By 1928, with the Oxley memorial still having not materialised, the Historical Society of Queensland existing virtually in name alone, and with veiled attempts at displacing him from the Centenary Fund, F.W.S. Cumbrae-Stewart's reign as intellectual force and prominent figure in the Brisbane elite, was beginning to take on water.

According to Peter Biskup and his essay on F.W.S., in 1928 Cumbrae-Stewart confided by letter in amateur historian and founder of the Royal Australian College of Surgeons in Queensland, Dr E. Sandford Jackson that the society had 'fallen on evil days. We have been unable to get a Secretary ... the subscriptions don't come in and only half a dozen members are financial ... I find that my work as Professor of Law takes all my time.'

Cumbrae-Stewart had published regular historical articles in the local *Brisbane Courier*. This reached its peak between 1924 and 1926, and included his nine-part weekly series on the history of Warrego.

Then these ceased. As Stewart writes: 'He said he had tried to keep the interest in Queensland history alive by writing articles in the *Brisbane Courier* [edited by Sanderson Taylor] but had fallen out with the editor and no longer were his articles being published.'

He held onto the presidency of the historical society until 1930, when he was replaced by the colourful and eccentric weather forecaster, Inigo Jones. Cumbrae-Stewart was vice-president for a couple more years before leaving the society altogether.

Then there was the question of his custodianship of the Oxley Memorial Trust funds which, as Manfred Cross has pointed out, Cumbrae-Stewart seemed to think was his own personal property.

When Cumbrae-Stewart refused to budge, a meeting held in 1929 and chaired by Brisbane Mayor William Jolly, accepted M.J. Barry's resignation from the trust. Jolly replaced him himself. Then in June 1930 another meeting — which Cumbrae-Stewart did not attend due to illness — appointed a new secretary and treasurer to the trust as well as a permanent committee of advisors. The next month the historical society passed a motion thanking F.W.S. 'for the care of historic relics etc. And enquire of him when it would be convenient to remove the society's belongings from the University'.

For Cumbrae-Stewart, his little Brisbane empire was being dismantled piece by piece. In 1935 Sir Raphael Cilento, then president of the society, noted that Cumbrae-Stewart 'severed his connection' with the group shortly after he was unseated as president. He was also 'taking with him' the funds of the memorial trust and announced 'that there was no further connection between this fund and the historical society'.

Cumbrae-Stewart took his marbles and left the playground, and he reserved a special enmity for Inigo Jones. He would later claim Jones was antagonistic towards the University of Queensland because they would not give him an honorary degree for his long range weather forecasting system.

But the scathed Cumbrae-Stewart got some small satisfaction regarding the trust. In early 1936 a retired grazier, P.M. Forrest, offered to sell his book collection to the Oxley Memorial Library. On March 9, 1936, Cumbrae-Stewart sent another of his handwritten letters to the mayor, by then Alfred Jones. He stressed the Forrest collection was essential to future Queenslanders. 'I am afraid that if we delay our consideration of Mr Forrest's very generous offer, the Oxley will miss a chance that will never come again.'

The price of the collection was £2447, almost the entire sum of the memorial fund. The mayor felt his hand was being forced, and he didn't like the idea of gutting the fund with a single purchase, but the sale went ahead.

It was cunning of Cumbrae-Stewart. He had emptied the war chest in a single move, denying his enemies crucial funds. By May 1936 he would give his last lecture, and be gone from the university by June.

The fatal blow to F.W.S.'s sizeable ego had already occurred, in 1935, when the University of Queensland decided to established a new School of Law, following a generous gift from entrepreneur T.C. Beirne. (The school is named after Beirne to this day.) The faculty was dramatically restructured, and F.W.S.'s role as Garrick Professor of Law would terminate in February 1936. He would then be employed on three-monthly contracts.

Cumbrae-Stewart was furious. He demanded from the university senate 12 months leave on full pay, which was not agreed to. He took at least one of the three-month contracts, then retired in May 1936.

F.W.S. and Zina were given numerous official farewells from Brisbane. It was like the departure of royalty. (Indeed there was a campaign mounted for Zina to receive Imperial Honours for her charity work. It was suggested she be made a 'Dame of the British Empire'. The damehood did not materialise.)

As the *Courier-Mail* reported, Zina offered a regal message to her adopted state on her farewell: 'Tell the women of Queensland I shall be following their work and watching their progress even though

I am not living among them in the future ...'

The university gave F.W.S. a mantel clock.

The couple left Brisbane for the United Kingdom aboard the *Nester* in June 1936. They would never return to the city. For 30 years F.W.S. had laid the groundwork for its history, and Zina had given it a moral compass. Then it all fell apart quite quickly, and they headed off to the bosom of Empire.

F.W.S. was ill on the trip, and he remained in poor health after the couple resettled in Melbourne, to be with their only son Frank, and died on March 24, 1938.

There are 'pictures of them leaving on their world trip after he retired, you see,' recalls June Cumbrae-Stewart. 'They went by sea to England. He had diabetes and he got very ill in Scotland, and they came back home to Melbourne because he was so ill, you see, and he died in Melbourne.

'He was quite attached to Brisbane.'

Had the Cumbrae-Stewarts become too big for their boots in little Brisbane? Or were they two people stuck in an Edwardian past who were rejected by an evolving modern city?

For a man who attempted so vigorously to put his stamp on a city, who wrote its history, contributed to its place names, even examined Queensland's legal borders, there are surprisingly few memories of him in today's Brisbane. There are his papers in the Fryer and John Oxley libraries, many of them donated by his daughter-in-law June Cumbrae-Stewart. In 1960 F.W.S.'s son Frank gave money to the university's Great Hall Appeal on its 50th anniversary, in memory of his father. There is a building named after Cumbrae-Stewart at the University of Queensland, opened in 1983.

There is the Scott Street flats, still owned by Zina's side of the family. Attached to the flats, now in the shadows of massive high-rise buildings, is a simple sign. *Zina Cumbrae-Stewart 1924.*

As for the Oxley obelisk, nobody is certain when it was put in place and unveiled. There appears to be no record of an official ceremony marking the event, nor any photographs.

The Brisbane City Council archives could find no trace of any unveiling date.

'I've looked for it too,' says Manfred Cross, 'and I couldn't find it.'

At some date after April 1928, the Oxley obelisk just appeared beside the Brisbane River.

And upon it are F.W.S. Cumbrae-Stewart's words cast in bronze. *Here John Oxley Landing to Look for Water Discovered the Site of this City. 28th September 1824.*

'F.W.S.'s interest in the Brisbane River was possibly because of having Scot house there,' says June. She means the Scott Street flats. 'Or he could have been interested in riparian rites down rivers or ... '

She isn't sure why Professor F.W.S. Cumbrae-Stewart had such a keen interest in the Brisbane River.

Once again I am contacted by relatives about the family history.

— No, during the 1974 flood of Brisbane the water did not submerge your grandmother's frangipani tree in the front yard. The water barely came up two feet. No, she was never under threat and asked to leave her house. Nor was she taken away in a tin rescue dinghy.

— No, we don't think you were stranded at her house during the flood.

— No, we cannot prove that Alf Clausen was working on Palm Island and incited the riots of 1930. He was a great fabricator and everything he said could have been lies. The photograph of him on Palm Island may not even be Palm Island, despite this being written on the back in pencil.

I speak with my childhood friend Bill about our canoeing trip to Goodna:

— No, he says. We did not set out close to the city, as you remember, but further down towards the mouth.

I speak with my father:

— No, you were not a little boy at your great-grandmother's funeral at Toowong. You were in your teens. In fact — were you there at all?

My entire remembered past in Brisbane suddenly shifts and shimmers.

A year after first standing before the John Oxley obelisk, and reading Field Book entries about the chain of ponds, I am contacted by a man called David Barr.

David has an interest in Oxley's true landing site, the original preferred location for the CBD, and has decided to find the chain of ponds in modern Brisbane.

'I do get to drive around south-east Queensland on a daily basis so I know the area reasonably well', he writes to me. 'One day last week I was in Bardon ... I thought the uppermost pond in the valley might be Norman Buchan Park below Government House.'

David's theory is that the 'beck' or stream and sequence of ponds, like lovely baubles on a string, that lured Oxley deeper into the fine valley, ran from present-day Gregory Park (Red Jacket Swamp) then between Beck and Elizabeth streets to the rear of the governor's grounds. He sends me a photograph of a lovely pond down by the governor's back fence. Could it be one of Oxley's ponds, still there only because it has been, for more than a century, untouched and protected inside the fences of the regal property?

'While in the area last week I had a look around', David continues. 'I found that under the [Norman Buchan] park there are three or four large concrete pipes, draining it. Now if you draw a line from there to a point between Beck and Elizabeth streets, I think you may have the course of the stream.'

I confirm with some Beck Street locals that some of the children of the area used to play near the pond and the large stormwater drains. One told me, 'When we were little we went into the drainpipes. They were huge. Well, big enough to walk through if you were a child. One day three of us entered the pipes at the bottom of Government House and followed it all the way through. It came out at the Milton Tennis Courts.'

The Milton courts. Formerly Frew Park. The *exact place*, hypothesised by historian Tom Truman in the 1950s, where Oxley came ashore and explored.

The pipes have followed the line of, indeed captured, the stream and Oxley's chain of ponds: David is right. The stream ran between Beck and Elizabeth Streets. Beck, meaning 'stream'. Directly beneath my grandparents' old house.

David goes even further. Now he's concentrating on the 'fine valley' that Oxley observed. 'I realised the Beck only went half way' into the supposed valley, David writes to me. 'So while in Paddington last week I had a look around upstream.'

A couple of weeks later he emails me a map. He believes he has ascertained the valley. He has tracked what he believes are the headwaters of the stream and its chain of ponds. He has discovered untouched and overgrown gullies deep in the heart of this patch of inner-city suburbia.

His map of the valley has at its southern border the ridge line that runs along the edge of the

Toowong Cemetery and Birdwood Terrace. The ridge curves north through Bardon, and its northern extremity is formed by present day Latrobe Terrace.

'I suggest this area is the headwater of our Beck', David says. 'I have noticed what could be a couple of tributaries along the way; to go any further west we would be over the ridge line into the Ithaca Creek catchment area.'

David tells me he is a truck driver, 'but I do have a translated copy of *The Anglo-Saxon Chronicles* on my bookshelf. I'm a £10 Pom from Yorkshire, came here in '64. Just about at my three score years and ten.'

His job gives him the opportunity 'to see all the lovely nooks and crannies' of south-east Queensland.

Almost two centuries after Oxley came ashore in his buckled leather boots, a Brisbane truck driver with a passion for history has drawn the city founder's vision from the modern landscape.

I'm astonished. Thrilled.

'I may be suggesting to you nothing new,' he says humbly. 'But on the other hand ...'

I have tried to get back to the Brisbane I used to know. This city teases you into believing it's possible. It offers a sequence of billowing curtains between past and present, and occasionally a parting emerges, and you put your arm through.

I have tried to find the index to the city. And just when I thought an approximation of it was starting to come together, it fell apart on me again and again.

I asked historian and former manager of the Royal Historical Society of Queensland, Allan Bell, now retired, what he thought of the proposition.

'Is Brisbane a book without an index?' he answered. 'No. The index exists in people's minds.'

I suspect Allan is right. There is the generation of dear Mrs Guy, the last of the elders still living in Beck Street, whose city came of age in the 1920s and '30s. It built its city hall. It paved its streets and sent an armada of trams out from the centre of the city beneath a spidery netting that gave the place form, coordinates, a fixed grid in the world. It was still a 'big country town' for many reasons. The tin-covered verandas of the unique Queenslander houses, well, you could find them in the CBD too, shading the footpaths, bringing the feel of the suburbs into the city, the city into the suburbs. So going 'to town' was just like walking down your own street. Could this have given the place its small town feeling to residents and visitors alike?

You had the Second World War, when the American generals moved in, and for a few brief years Brisbane felt like an important centre, a place that would matter to history. Then they all moved away, and it became Brisbane again, the quiet river city with its stupefying heat and humidity, its cake stalls in Queen Street, its gas oven exhibitions in city hall, its rowdy market in Roma Street, its dances up at Cloudland where the parents of much of the city's next generation first met. Cloudland, a little shelled ear of concrete on a ridge in Bowen Hills, that was torn down in the dark of night to make way for an unremarkable string of brick flats, torn down on the orders of a government that didn't care for the city's index, let alone its book.

Then you had the '60s, and a mayor who decided the small town had to go up and out. Skyscrapers. Freeways. Let's get Brisbane in step with the world. The trams gave way to the car. The car needed more roads. The roads then started to erase the character.

The peanut farmer in charge of the state famously used to sit in his office not far from where the city's convicts were flogged to within an inch of their lives and count the construction cranes outside the office windows. ('I often thought Joh did not pull down the Commissariat Store [the city's oldest building] because he could not see it from his office,' says Allan Bell.) And despite all this modernisation, the city could still not shuck off its country-town mantle. Was it the peanut farmer? Presiding over the city just as those moneyed squatters used to do in the settlement right from the start? Was it a state of mind that inhibited the city? That turned its vision inward?

Then you had the World Exposition of 1988, an event repeatedly cited as the birth of the New Brisbane. The world came to the city, just as the Americans had come during the war. But what was different? They cleared the southern bank of the river across from the CBD, razed the old pubs and brothels and mercantile stores for the show. They had a fun fair that, in hindsight, did not show off the city to the planet, but inadvertently showed the people of Brisbane what cosmopolitanism was, how others lived, how it worked in more worldly cities. Multiculturalism was good, so was eating outdoors, drinking with different nationalities, staying up late. Brisbane hadn't had this under the peanut farmer, and now they saw that their city perfectly suited *carnivale*, that it didn't have to be drab and wowserish, that it had a lot to offer. The Exposition itself didn't transform the city. But it changed the city's collective state of mind.

During the six-month Expo in 1988 the Fitzgerald Inquiry into police corruption was continuing its sittings across the river in the CBD, having begun the year before. So on the South Bank of the river the Skyneedle strafed the city by night and thousands travelled about the site in the specially built monorail and locals and visitors poked their head into the Nepalese Peace Pagoda, enjoyed more than 100 pavilions and packed into the piazzas to witness circus, mime and acrobat acts – while generations of graft and corruption were being steadily dismantled in the Law Courts Building in George Street. The peanut farmer had been deposed at the end of 1987 after two decades in office, and the inquiry would continue until 1989, taking with it all sorts of casualties, from ministers to police commissioners. It was a broom that would sweep through the course of Queensland history.

Could Expo and the Inquiry have somehow

coalesced in the minds of Brisbane people and given the city a fresh start? Did this change the city as powerfully as the peanut farmer's bulldozers?

Then you had a wave of interstate and international migration to Brisbane that became a tsunami. Another premier deemed Queensland the Smart State. The city began attracting world-class minds in biotechnology and medical research. The city universities started swelling with overseas students attracted to this smart city with a lovely climate. Then it built a world-class modern art gallery, and refashioned its State Library into the best of its type in the country, and built more bridges across the river. 'It's brother and sister to me, and aunts, and company, and food and drink, and (naturally) washing. It's my world, and I don't want any other,' said Rat.

And now? What now? It is a giant construction site trying to facilitate its expanding population. It's a city losing trees and 'character' housing to infrastructure. It is a city slowly but steadily surrendering its uniqueness to accommodate the people, many of whom came here for that very uniqueness.

It is a CBD with glass towers and sushi bars and globally familiar fashion outlets and suits and punks and police and buskers and schoolchildren and eccentrics and Goths and skateboarders and old ladies walking with umbrellas against the sun and young families and drunks and backpackers listening to iPods and teenagers clustering outside fast food joints and businessmen striking deals in fine bright restaurants on the river at Eagle Street Pier and multi-millionaire city identities living in their penthouse roosts overlooking the Story Bridge and revellers in imitation paddle steamers on the river and lovers quarrelling in the old Botanic Gardens not far from the gallery dedicated to painter William Robinson in Old Government House where Governor Bowen lived and where, now, you can see pictures that reach for the meaning of life itself, and politicians that come and go brawling in the parliamentary chamber at the end of George Street, and 7-Eleven stores where there used to be old tea rooms and leather repair stores, and taverns from the '80s that were once the epicentre of cool and are now dark caverns for daytime drinkers and gamblers, and low brick and sandstone office buildings still standing below the towers, with names and telephone numbers from another era fading in the sun, and gay pubs when there used to be none, and office workers all wearing their lanyards, and people packing the air-conditioned food halls in the middle of the day, and the city emptying at night, and people sitting at home, young and new to town, who have never even wandered past the Commissariat Store, let alone understood its importance, people who haven't yet been able to put the city hall in the context of the city's two-century narrative, and Customs House, and the old windmill, and the Treasury, and the statue of Queen Victoria, and the lions in King George Square, and the Story Bridge, and the little chapel next to St Stephen's Cathedral, and the old Brisbane residents in their creaky, lopsided Queenslanders in suburbs that were once a decent tram ride to town, and are now part of the roaring inner-city, who are dying out and taking deep, deep connections to the city with them.

Just like any other city.

Then one day the boy, having been swept away from the city all those years ago, returned when he was an older man.

He went out to the house built above the giant boulders as big as dinosaur eggs, to see if there was anything left of that life. He peered in under the house where he had built his city in the cool earth, and it had gone. He looked up to the floorboards of the house and saw, chalked on a beam, his family's surname. Still there, forty years later, scrawled by a timber merchant before the beam was delivered to the street for the building of the house.

Now, with his own boy and a little girl, he looked for the index to the city. It was not in the old house above the boulders. But it had to be somewhere.

So again, one morning at the end of summer, he journeyed out to the Toowong Cemetery, formerly know as the Brisbane General Cemetery. It had once been outside the city limits, but was now a 43.73-hectare necropolis just 4.5 kilometres west of the CBD, surrounded by suburbs and streets and freeways.

He had been here with his boy, looking for relatives, and now he had more people from his past to find. Especially his great-great-grandmother Ellen, who had died of dementia and a broken neck and pneumonia. If he could find her, it might go some way towards starting this index of his.

He found it a very pretty cemetery, with its plethora of fig trees, bunya and cypress pines, jacaranda, camphor laurels and eucalypts. He could see how people might come here just to take a stroll and catch their thoughts.

The Brisbane-born writer Thea Astley always remembered her parents fighting on family outings to various city parks. They often visited the Toowong Cemetery. He remembered a short story of hers, called 'Coming of Age', about a young girl's introduction to the perils of adult life:

'We enjoyed the cemeteries too. I think they must have been Depression-era entertainment, cheap and instructive. Or maybe my mother had a fanatical wish to impress on us the evanescence of things temporal. I had a completely balanced attitude to graveyards on those hot summer afternoons as I leapt slab to slab. Sometimes I'd pause and read aloud life histories that were frighteningly long or brief, but the temporary condition in which my thin, agile smallgirl body jumped and hopped was moved only by the eternal charm of well-tended lawns and concrete angels with adorable smiles.'

Now after a couple of hours on this hot morning the man, who was the boy, realised that the cemetery was, in a sense, the story of Brisbane. It was hilly and riven with gullies. It had a watercourse that ran through the middle of it. It was thick with shrubs and trees. It was hemmed in on all sides by traffic.

On the high ridges rested the elite of the city: politicians, barristers, public servants. On the slopes, the unremarkable middle-class. And down on the floors of the little valleys, the paupers and criminals. It was like that, too, beyond the borders of the cemetery.

The man clambered up to the towering obelisk on the highest knoll. This was the grave and memorial to Queensland's second governor, Samuel Wensley Blackall – the cemetery's first burial, on January 3, 1871.

Nearby he found Samuel Walker Griffith, chief justice and Queensland premier. In the late 1800s Griffith fought corruption, encouraged immigration and opposed the squattocracy embedded in Brisbane. He was pro-Federation and drafted much of the Bill that formed the Australian constitution.

The man stood before Griffith's grave. Its white marble cross, cracked in two places, rested on pine needles beside the plinth. Screwed into the stone base of the grave was a small brass plaque – *Maintained by the Queensland Government.*

Nearby he found Thomas Glassey, a humanitarian and agitator who served in the first federal parliament in 1901. He would have known Griffith. Not far away was Sir Joshua Bell, the politician and squatter who had a few run-ins with Governor Bowen. Close by too was Sir Arthur Palmer, lieutenant governor and president of the legislative assembly. He died on March 20, 1898, and was granted a state funeral. But he'd wished for a private ceremony, so the government acquiesced, and his family brought him here to the high knoll the following afternoon and buried him.

Then the man wandered a short distance down the eastern flank of the knoll and visited Thomas Pennington Lucas, doctor and writer and inventor of a magic papaw ointment. He had published a novel about Brisbane in the year 2000, when Bengal tigers roamed the riverbanks and the city lay in ruins, victim of its own insatiable lust and greed.

He studied the headstone for Dr Lucas and that of his wife Susan. *In Loving Memory of My Dear Husband*, it read. *Dr Thomas P. Lucas. November 15, 1917.* Also on the headstone is *Susan, died October 30, 1933.*

But a newer plaque sat on the grave too, dedicated to Mary Bradbury Lucas, the doctor's second wife, Irene Mary Lucas, their daughter, and Harold Ernest, their six-year-old son. Mary had died in childbirth in 1888, and baby Irene lived just one month. Harold died in 1890.

Why the new, belated plaque, with a modern manufacturer's sticker still affixed to it, so close to the headstone of Thomas and Susan which carried an image of each? Had Thomas been buried with his second wife and their children in 1917? And then had Susan erected a new tombstone that not only waited for her name, when she joined her husband in eternity, but obliterated the existence of the earlier wife? A relative would later allege that young Harold suffered physical injuries and may have been 'murdered' by Susan. Stories, the man thought, don't end, not even in death.

Down the laneway from Dr Lucas he paid his respects to Carl A. Feilberg, former editor of the *Brisbane Courier*, who died suddenly in 1887. 'He had been suffering four months from spasmodic asthma, the immediate cause of death was failure of the action of the heart', wrote the *Sydney Morning Herald*. He was lauded in Parliament House down in George Street: 'As an editor he was free from prejudice, but inclined to be rather exacting in his demand for consistency and integrity in public men, while desirous of treating members of both political parties with scrupulous fairness.'

Lower down the slope he bumped into Thomas

Dowse. Poor Thomas. Brisbane's first journalist. A horse trader. A former convict. The Samuel Pepys of Brisbane. Here he rested in a poor man's grave, the cross snapped off, his name barely legible, the ground of the grave sunken, the weeds dead, the little low fence around him cracked. Poor Thomas Dowse.

Wandering onto lower ground he came across James Young, died in 1904, the builder and owner of the house 'Lucerne', which, these days, the man jogged past most mornings on his way to the running track beside the river. And John Melville, survivor of the 1855-56 Sir Augustus Gregory expedition to northern Australia, and long-time curator of the cemetery itself. And Captain Almond, Brisbane Port Master. And Thomas Finney, department store mogul. And William Dart, a sugar pioneer and entrepreneur who planted cotton and bananas on the river flats near the present-day University of Queensland boatsheds. And Thomas Rochester, just 18 and dead in a boating accident at Redcliffe in 1919.

The man wandered and wandered, and found the narrow, humble grave of Mayor William Jolly. He paid his respects to Arthur Hoey Davis, aka Steele Rudd, prolific writer. He found by accident the former Queensland politician Leonard Eastment, who'd lived at the top of Beck Street, and stored his grandfather's election signs under his house.

He came across Robert Henry Monteith, who enlisted with the Australian Imperial Force on May 31, 1915, in Brisbane and died in action on September 2, 1918. By December his father Henry, of Ironside near St Lucia, was writing to the Defence Department in Melbourne seeking details of his son's final movements. 'I am sorry to put you to so much trouble', Henry wrote, 'but for family reasons I am very anxious to have all these particulars as soon as possible.'

Not far from Robert the man stood before the memorial to Leslie Norman Collin, *killed in action, Gallipoli, 9 May, 1915*. He was 21.

His father, William Collin, was a prominent shipping agent in Brisbane, and he had been writing to the Secretary of Defence through the latter half of 1915 trying to find the whereabouts of his son. Letters from father to son had been returned. Then in January of the following year a witness to young Collin's death – George Boulton of Brisbane – gave a written statement: 'After leaving Egypt I next saw the said Lieutenant Leslie Norman Collin at Quinn's Post Gallipoli on the Seventh day of May 1915 and saluted him.' He next saw Collin on

May 10, 'lying dead between forty and fifty yards in front of the trenches at Quinn's Post aforesaid. When I saw the body … I turned the body over and I am positive he was dead as there was absolutely no sign of life. I was working for about two hours in and around the body of the said Lieutenant Leslie Norman Collin and during that time no sign of life appeared.' He said it appeared Collin 'had been shot on the left side near the heart'.

It was all here, the man thought. The city. The stories. They extended from the founding of the settlement to the city's growth to the immigrant wave to the politicians and journalists in the 19th century to the entrepreneurs and lawmakers and railway commissioners and soldiers and carpenters and paupers and victims of disease and mishap and broken hearts.

Then he went to look for his great-great-grandmother. He had already been unable to find the Foxes, over by the fence right beside the freeway that headed into the city's western corridor towards Ipswich. They simply weren't there.

Then he went down into the valley not far from the soggy creek bed that cut through the cemetery, through the necropolis, and she wasn't there either. He tramped about the sodden earth beneath the eucalypts for half an hour, and he couldn't find any sign of Ellen. She didn't exist.

He felt defeated, climbing back up to the top of the knoll. He felt defeated by the cemetery and the exact grave coordinates he was able to retrieve on his computer – the Portion, Section and Grave Number.

On the ground he was only able to find the Portion markers. There was nothing to indicate the sections, nor the grave numbers. Many of the headstones were broken or just missing. Nothing was organised, coordinated, legible. Without an index, the book fell apart.

The man stood on top of the high knoll. He heard the breeze through the hoop pines. He saw dark clouds moving over towards the city. And from this vantage point he could see the skyscrapers of the metropolis itself. Bright. Sharp-edged. Made of glass and mirrors that carried reflections of other buildings and, depending on where you were standing, the clouds too.

He stood quietly and looked at the city for a long time. His past was all around but nowhere. It had disappeared into the hill folds, the great sticky canopies of mango trees, the dark shadows under wooden houses.

It was the city where he had been a child. A happy kingdom where he had played in the rain, crashed his bicycle and tumbled over the handlebars, put on a cape and jumped off the back landing, looked at the moon and knew a man had stood on it that morning, learned how to read and write, laughed and cried and dreamt.

The man gazed towards Paddington. His own children, born in Brisbane, were over there in the house not far from the chain of ponds. They were scratching in the soil in the backyard, observing patterns on the wooden floorboards made by the sunlight through the kitchen window, drawing crude trees and animals and people and the stars and the moon in a scrapbook. They were making their own memories now.

This city was theirs too. The little city of wooden off-cuts and seedling containers and the muddy, serpentine river of tap water.

He had been born here. This was his home.

Brisbane.

Bibliography and Acknowledgements

All reasonable efforts were taken to obtain permission to use copyright material reproduced in this book, but in some cases copyright holders could not be traced. The author welcomes information in this regard.

Thanks are due to the copyright holders of the following books, articles and lectures, listed here in the order in which my narrative progresses:

The Brisbane Centenary Official Historical Souvenir, Watson, Ferguson & Co, Brisbane, 1924.

Steele, J.G., *The Explorers of the Moreton Bay District 1770–1830*, University of Queensland Press, 1972.

The original manuscripts of John Oxley's Field Books, which are held in the Mitchell Library, Sydney.

Truman, T.C., 'Rewriting the History of the Birth of Brisbane', *Courier-Mail*, April/May 1950.

Gregory, Helen, *The Brisbane River Story*, Australian Maritime Conservation Society Inc., 1996.

Malouf, David, 'A First Place: A Mapping of the World'. Delivered as the 14th Herbert Blaiklock Memorial Lecture on September 26, 1984, and published in *Southerly* 45 (1985).

Malouf, David, 'Dream Stuff', from *Dream Stuff*, Chatto & Windus, 2000.

Much of the background information relating to the history of the Brisbane City Hall clock was taken from research articles produced by the First Queensland Chapter of the National Association of Watch and Clock Collectors, and two articles: 'The Synchronomes at the End of the World, Part One' by Norman Heckenberg and Anthony Roberts, *Horological Journal*, October 2006; and 'The Synchronomes at the End of the World, Part Two', by Norman Heckenberg and Anthony Roberts, *Horological Journal*, November 2006.

Condon, Matthew, 'Matthew's Passion', *Good Weekend* magazine, August 24, 1996.

Stewart, Jean, *Scribblers, A Ladies' Literary Society in Brisbane 1911*, J. and D. Stewart, Brisbane, 2007.

The thumbnail portraits of F.W.S. Cumbrae-Stewart on page 69 come from 'Cumbrae-Stewart, Francis William Sutton (1865–1938)', *Australian Dictionary of Biography*, by Harrison Bryan, Volume 8, Melbourne University Press, 1981; and *Vivant Professores, distinguished members of the University of Queensland, 1910–1940*, by Helen Gregory, Fryer Memorial Library, Occasional Publication No. 7, 1987.

Biskup, Peter, 'The Politics of Preserving the Past: The Early Years of the Historical Society of Queensland', *Journal of the Royal Historical Society of Queensland*, Volume XIII, No. 8, November 1988.

The quotes by castaway Thomas Pamphlet are taken from 'Narrative of Thomas Pamphlet', reproduced in J.G. Steele's *The Explorers of the Moreton Bay District 1770–1830*.

Petrie, Constance Campbell, *Tom Petrie's Reminiscences of Early Queensland*, Watson, Ferguson & Co., Brisbane, 1904.

Quotes from the letters of Dalipie and Dalinkua taken from the *Moreton Bay Courier*: November 17, 1858; November 24, 1858; December 11, 1858; January 8, 1859; January 26, 1859.

Quote about Dalipie and Dalinkua taken from

Making Links, a research project by Aboriginal and Torres Strait Islander students from Cleveland State High School, Kelvin Grove State High School, Saint James Prac., Brisbane, 1995.

Cumbrae-Stewart, F.W.S., *Queenslander* magazine, December 1, 1923.

Parker, Gilbert, *Round the Compass of Australia*, E.W.Cole, Melbourne, 1892.

Johnston, W. Ross, *Brisbane, The First Thirty Years*, Boolarong Publications, 1988.

Quote from 'Smart Cities: Rethinking the City Centre', Smart State Council, Queensland Government, May 2007.

Knight, J.J., *In the Early Days: History and Incident of Pioneer Queensland*, Sapsford & Co., Brisbane, 1895.

Ross, William, *The Fell Tyrant*, Ward, London, 1836.

Noble, Louise, 'Re-reading the City: Indigenous Geography and Colonial Space in the Australian City'; paper delivered on September 27, 2006, to the Subtropical Cities 2006 conference, Brisbane.

Condon, Matthew, extracts from 'Free at Last', *Qweekend, Courier-Mail*, June 6, 2009.

Quotes from Glyn Davis on Queensland's Letters-

Patent taken from the web page 'Document-ing a Democracy – Australia's Story' on the National Archives of Australia website.

My thanks to Darryl Jones, Associate Profes-sor and Deputy Director of the Environment Futures Centre and the Griffith School of Environment, Griffith University, Brisbane, for thoughts on brush turkeys and their place in Brisbane city, emailed to me October 1, 2009.

Burns, Kathryn E., 'This Other Eden: Exploring a Sense of Place in Twentieth-Century Recon-structions of Australian Childhoods', thesis, University of Sydney, October 2006.

Trollope, Anthony, *Australia and New Zealand*, (Aus-tralian edition) George Robertson, Melbourne, 1873.

Bjelke-Petersen, Joh, *Don't You Worry About That!*, Angus & Robertson, 1990.

Schultz, Julianne, 'The Tail That Wagged the Dog', *Griffith Review*, 'Hidden Queensland' issue, Spring 2008.

Curnow, Hugh, 'All Done with Mirrors', *The Bul-letin*, November 7, 1964.

Smith, Sue, 'Spotlight on Sibley', *Courier-Mail*, August 24, 1993.

Lucas, T.P., *The Curse and its Cure* (in two volumes),

J.H. Reynolds, Brisbane, 1894.

Condon, Matthew, extracts from 'Toys in the Attic', *Qweekend, Courier-Mail*, July 28, 2007.

Quotes taken from *The Journal of the Royal Historical Society of Queensland*, October 1925.

Travers, Ben, *94 Declared: Cricket Reminiscences*, Elm Tree Books, 1981.

Quotes from *The Burra Charter: The Australia ICOMOS Charter for Places of Cultural Significance 1999*.

Quotes on Brisbane architecture and heritage taken from Doug Hall's essay 'Restoring Queensland's Colonial Past', unpublished, 2010.

My thanks to the *Courier-Mail*, Brisbane, for permission to quote from news stories relating to the growth of the city and its infrastructure.

Astley, Thea, *A Descant for Gossips*, Angus & Robertson, 1960.

Astley, Thea, *The Multiple Effects of Rainshadow*, Penguin Books Australia, 1997.

Baker, Candida, *Yacker, Australian Writers Talk About Their Work*, Picador, 1986.

The section on the Springboks tour of Brisbane in 1971 was informed by 'Springbok Tour Confrontation' by Raymond Evans in *Radical Brisbane, An Unruly History*, edited by Raymond

Evans and Carole Ferrier, The Vulgar Press, 2004.

Stewart, Jean, *Scribblers, A Ladies' Literary Society in Brisbane 1911*, J. and D. Stewart, Brisbane, 2007.

My sincere thanks to David Barr for sharing his investigations into the source of John Oxley's 'chain of ponds'.

Astley, Thea, 'Coming of Age', *Collected Stories*, UQP, 1997.

The military records and correspondence regarding the deaths of Robert Henry Monteith and Leslie Norman Collin were retrieved from the online database Army – World War I – at the National Archives of Australia website.

Brisbane never set out to be a comprehensive history of the city, but many of its segments were inspired and underpinned by the excellent work of local historians who have been tilling the Brisbane soil for decades.

I am indebted to the works and cooperation of Jean Stewart, Rod Fisher, Raymond Evans, J.G. Steele, W. Ross Johnston and Helen Gregory. Rod

Fisher's *Boosting Brisbane, Imprinting the Colonial Capital of Queensland* (Boolarong Press, Brisbane, 2009) and *Sites of Separation* (Boolarong Press, Brisbane, 2009) were indispensable guides to colonial Brisbane. Thank you also to the continuing work of the Brisbane History Group.

I also want to pay tribute to: Annabel Lloyd, Brisbane City Council Archives Coordinator and the archive staff for welcoming me to their Brisbane City Archive facilities at Moorooka; the staff of the Fryer Library and the State Library of Queensland, Brisbane, and in particular Dianne Byrne, Original Materials Librarian with the State Library's Heritage Collection; Sue Finnigan and Dr Valerie Dennis of the National Trust of Queensland; the staff and volunteers of the Royal Historical Society of Queensland; Brisbane City Council historian Brian Rough; the staff of Old Government House, Gardens Point and Government House at Rosalie. I would especially like to thank Queensland Newspapers Chief Librarian Rosemary Kunst, *Qweekend* editor Christine Middap, *Courier-Mail* Editor-in-Chief David Fagan, and the staff of both publications.

Brisbane contains passages relating to the late F.W.S. Cumbrae-Stewart and his association with the Oxley Memorial Trust in the 1920s and '30s. While Cumbrae-Stewart's engagement with the John Oxley memorial obelisk is examined at length, that other fine product of the Trust's vision – the John Oxley Library – is not. The library opened its doors in 1934 and has evolved into Queensland's preeminent guardian of the state and Brisbane city's historical documents and ephemera. It is a vibrant testament to the foresight of Cumbrae-Stewart and his colleagues.

I would also like to acknowledge the staff of the Australian Newspapers Digitisation Program, a monolithic project within the National Library of Australia. Your incredible work has been of immense value.

I owe a debt to the Friends of Toowong Cemetery for their ongoing dedication to Queensland's most important burial ground in inner-city Brisbane. The Brisbane City Council gained control of the city's public cemeteries in 1930 and since 2004 has provided an online search facility for records of the dead, including aerial photographs of grave locations produced by spatial data company Qasco.

Many Brisbane novelists and poets provided inspiration for the book, and I would like to pay homage to Rodney Hall, David Robotham, David

Malouf, Gerard Lee, Jessica Anderson, Gwen Harwood, Janette Turner Hospital, Georgia Savage and Peter Porter. I particularly wish to salute the memory of that great Australian writer, Thea Astley. Additional thanks is offered to Dr Laurie Hergenhan, Emeritus Professor of Australian Literature at the University of Queensland.

The book was informed by several interviews with numerous people and I am grateful for their cooperation. Thank you to Rodney Hall, Peter Beattie, Brisbane Lord Mayor Campbell Newman, Andrew Sibley, Alex Bond, Robin Gibson, David Rowbotham, Manfred Cross, Doug Hall and the late Clem Jones. Sincere thanks also to Dr June Cumbrae-Stewart.

Phillipa (Pip) McGuinness, Executive Publisher of UNSW Press/New South, first proposed I tackle the subject of my home city and sent me on this odyssey, so thank you, Pip. I am grateful also to Dr Heather Cam, managing editor of UNSW Press. *Brisbane* was granted the great good fortune to be edited by the wonderful Judith Lukin-Amundsen, citizen of the city, and benefited hugely from her expertise. Thank you, Judith.

I owe an enormous amount to various branches of my family, especially my parents Karen and Ron

Condon, and Allan Miles and Marion Thomas. The book, too, is a tribute to those relatives who carved out a life in the city since the beginning of the 20th century, often against tremendous odds. It is, in a small way, a testimony to them: in particular, Freda Miles, George Baker, Bill Condon, and Kathleen Condon.

Finally, I would like to offer my love and heartfelt thanks to my wife, Kate, and my children, Finnigan and Bridie Rose. *Brisbane* is for you.

ALDERLEY
Wardell Street
THE GAP
Waterworks Road
PADD
Government House
Beck S
ROSALIE
Sir Samuel Griffith Drive
Toowong
Cemetery
MILT
Mt. Coot-tha
Western Freeway
BRISB
Moggill Road
KENMORE
Ha
GOODNA